The Catalan Poems

Pere Gimferrer (Barcelona, 1945) is the author of more than thirty books in Catalan and Spanish. A member of the Real Academia Española and the Acadèmia de Bones Lletres de Barcelona, he has won numerous accolades for his work, including Spain's National Poetry Prize and the Ramon Llull Prize for the Novel.

Adrian Nathan West is a translator and critic and author of *The Aesthetics of Degradation*.

T0288240

PERE GIMFERRER

The Catalan Poems

Translated by Adrian Nathan West

CARCANET

First published in Great Britain in 2019 by
Carcanet Press Ltd
Alliance House, 30 Cross Street
Manchester M2 7AQ
www.carcanet.co.uk

This publication was supported by a grant from the Institut Ramon Llull.

A CIP catalogue record for this book is available from the British Library.
ISBN 978 1 784107 67 3

Typeset by XL Publishing Services, Exmouth
Printed & bound in England by SRP Ltd.

The publisher acknowledges financial assistance
from Arts Council England.

Contents

From *The Mirrors*

Snares   1
Systems   3
Second Vision of March   4
Tropic of Capricorn   7
Now the Poet Undertakes a Practical Act   11

From *The Darkening Hour*

Distant   12

From *Blind Fire*

Elegy   14
Vlad Drakul   16
Blind Fire   19
May   22
Solstice   23

Three Poems

Vision   24
Unity   27
Night in April   28

From *Deserted Space*   30

Two Homages

Light of Velintonia   45
Land of Antoni Tàpies   46

From *Apparitions*   47

As an Epilogue

Time   54
Winter   55
Poetic Art   56
Sculpture   57
Fate   58
Memories   59
Vigil   60
Landscape   61
Death   62
Philistines   63
Afterward   64
Bell   65
Midday   66
Desire   67
Sign   68

From *The Tempest*

Spectacle   69
Exile   70
The Gloaming Hour   71
Plaint   72

From *Light*

Apotheosis   73
Stalking   74
Testament   75
Ceremonies   76
End   77

From *Uncollected Poems*

Evening 78
Morn 79
Compact 80

From *The Castle of Purity*

Lay 81

From the *Dietari*

The Poet and the Dictator 83
I am Still Learning 84
A Sorcerer's Disappearance 85
A Russian in Paris 87
The Enemy Within 89
A Toast 91
Simulacra 93
Facts and Morals 95
The American Poet 97
The Pistol and the Drawing Rooms 99
The Mulatta and the Dandy 101
The Bedroom of the Poetess 104
Beginnings 106
Le Carré and Simenon 108
The Only Emperor 110
A Sunday in April 112
A Gentleman in Majorca 114
The Secrets of Plagiarism 116
Twilight 118
Musil, the Spectator 120
Witches in Venice 122

An Interview with Pere Gimerrer 125

Index of Titles 131

Snares

Poetry is the subject of the poem
WALLACE STEVENS

I

They say Apollinaire wrote
culling scraps of conversation
overheard in cafes in Montmartre: cubist perspectives,
like the clippings in the journal of Juan Gris,
                              snares
where the backdrop is sharper than the cynosure,
the foreground a bit disfigured, reduced to angles and spirals – the
     colours livelier in twilit windows: a clang
in the cabin of childhood – Hölderlin talked of that,
they were chambers: preceptor, red damask, Venetian mirror,
Wozu dichter in dürftiger Zeit, and Goethe would write Schiller that
     his young friend,
though still a bit timid and, naturally, wanting in experience
(everything in that letter's tone makes manifest the older man's
     benevolent contempt for the poetry of the younger: he had already
     written verses – so it struck him – far serener, or better, or if not, of
     a classicism such as would vouchsafe his immortality)
because classic art is imperishable: Hölderlin, in his late years, wrote
     to his mother
respectfully, with turns of phrase he had learned as a boy,
asking only for underwear, a pair of badly darned socks, small
     commonplace things,
like Rimbaud in Abyssinia, or at the sickhouse
     – *Que je suis donc devenu malheureux!* –
And so poets end: injured, annulled, dead-alive, and hence we call
     them poets.
And so? The crucifixion of a few is perhaps no more than a sign
and grandeur and death the equilibrium of others,
and Yeats's phosphorescence (Byzantium, like a gong at twilight) the
     price to be paid

for him whose name was writ in water.

Because a price must be paid, you can be sure of it: Eurydice still lies
    dead

over the circuits and the blue of a room tepid like the carcass of a
    mahogany piano.

Orpheus's world is that of the mirror's backing: Orpheus's fall,

like Eurydice's journey home from Hell, the bicycles, the boys
    chewing gum on their way back from playing tennis,

backs red, bodies golden – and fragile – the girls in red leggings with
    Adriatic blue eyes sipping gin and orange,

the ones who swam nude in the novels of Pavese, and we dubbed them
    the topolino girls

(I'm not sure you know the topolino: it was a car fashionable, or
    maybe just often to be seen, in the *roaring forties*).

But I'm older now, even if old is not quite the right word, but the
    colour of gin and orange

où sont où sont the dreams that money can buy?

II

This poem is
a succession of snares: for
reader and
proofreader
and for the editor of the poem.
        To be clear,
no one has told me what
the snares conceal, because
that would be like telling me the figure
in the carpet, and this, as
James has made clear, is not
possible.

From *The Mirrors* (Els miralls, 1970)

Systems

Poetry is
a system of rotating
mirrors, gliding harmoniously,
displacing light and shadow in the dressing room: why
the ground glass? As if talking – conversing
with tablecloths and soft music – I were to say to you, my love,
that this or that reflex is the poem,
or an aspect of it: a poem may be written
about the dead Duchess of Yekaterinburg,
and when the sun sinks red in the windows, I recall
her blue eyes… I don't know, I've spent such long hours
on night trains reading crime novels
(alone in the empty house, we opened the armoires)
and one night, on the way to Berna, two men kissed in my car
because it was empty, or I was asleep, or it was dark
(hand seeks for hand, body for body)
                              and now the glass turns
and this aspect is hidden: real and fictitious,
convention, in other words, and the things we have lived,
the experience of light in the wintertide forests,
the strain of imposing coherence – it is mirror play –
the acts that dissolve in irreality,
the yellow, the leprosy, rust; the moss that blots images,
the tar slathering the faces of the boys in *canotiers*,
all that died one afternoon with the bicycles,
chrome reds submerged in the cisterns
bodies (in space as in time) in slow motion beneath the waters.
(Dark like the backing of a mirror in shards, the dressing room is the
    axis of this poem.)

From *The Mirrors* (Els miralls, 1970)   3

Second Vision of March

I

People in the darkest of purlieus
with streetlamps and soot – boys who scrub chimneys by night with
    warm hands
and scrawl Paleolithic inscriptions on the blighted walls of the
    orphanage – a chamois, a serpent, the death of a mare –
and kiss and die under streetlamps at knifepoint with *claqué*
and the fog sops their top hats when it thickens – all oil and smoke in
    those homes in the port
where the white necklines rest, and the blood of the marquees, and
    the marriage beds,
the accordion of the *bals-musette*, its mistress a bit withered,
    blond dye-job very shoddy – but her blue eyes quite young –
    smoking Gauloises,
and now, with nightfall,
the flame from the *becs de gaz*,
                       like the lips of a woman
    who kisses my eyelids,
because eyes only close for death or for love.

II

It's cold in the darkest of purlieus, and still people think
of the felt hat and the Browning with rubber grips in the pocket,
because not on the first two corners, but on the third, a fist blow will
    shatter the glass
and the girls playing in the alley, as in an old Chaplin film
– blonde, drab jerseys, eyes the colour of sea pearl –
stifled by ribbon and lace and the murk of the metro,
when the Carrer d'Aribau was like a clip from a postwar newsreel
(the girls entombed in the Fossar de les Moreres, with the lonelyhearts
    column and the scent of starch in the kitchen – the after-dinner

                    From *The Mirrors* (Els miralls, 1970)

radio, like a voice from the land of the dead),
spirit, my spirit, who called you to a wisteria summer?

III

Like men made whole by action, or desire,
    or a warm body in the depths of a narrow lane,
in the depths of a diorama like back in Colón,
    showing the discovery of America, in period-piece style,
    remindful of the century before –
the paper of the agaves still shifted a bit, brushed with a green dragon
    flashing fangs *in extremis* –
and all into the canoe – we furrowers of the black waters of Lethe.
So, for a time, the poem suffers the imperious necessity of designating
    the real
and cannot do so: is obliged to periphrasis
to allude to the transit of a summer cloud,
to the warm corolla fraying on the lips,
to the sense of nostalgia, to fear, to contact with the brume of memory,
the poem's making and unmaking, the loss of contact with consciousness
that awaits us at a cocktail party – and already, that man in the tuxedo
is dead like an actor on the screen.
There, where word will become snare
but only so far as we wish: whether ashes or music,
it remains, perhaps, an effort of lucidity, and its simultaneity of planes
corresponds to the intricacy of experience: to wit,
there is no other way to explain that instant
between two stations, departing from Salzburg
with the lights and the tracks – a ground level shot of a child playing
    amid vapor – glum, glum,
and only a poem can explain the wherefores of those princely eyes on
    that lush with the five o' clock shadow.
A world's unmaking: that is grandeur,
fall who may, be it a vamp in mink furs or a classmate we remember
    nothing of save that his hands shook beneath his desk one summer
    afternoon.

From *The Mirrors* (Els miralls, 1970)   5

IV

I have never lived the distance between what we wish to say and say,
the futility of grasping the tension of language, of conceiving
    a system of acts and words,
a body of relations between the poem as written and read.
It may be an Elotian discourse at times, I think
this poem puts in danger
one of the levels of my poetry: that is to say, this discourse shows here,
    all at once, the two faces of the mirror.
                              I close it and it spins:
at night, lit bright in the gilded gloom, on the streets or in death,
like the rustling of the forest and its trees that fall in silence
– where, if not in my heart?

From *The Mirrors* (Els miralls, 1970)

Tropic of Capricorn

It was the first year you heard records on the beach played through
    speakers.
In the coffeehouses, no one talked politics, and all the men carried
    canes.
I can still see the red-fringed tablecloths before me.
After lunch, we had all fallen silent – you know those silences
that surge up in the midst of discussion, when the sun glints on the
    glasses.
Your mother was twenty-seven, and was chatting with Pilar about
how to mend some dress or other, because soon, the girl would
soon be starting school.
                        You don't remember,
but people on the street looked different – not like later on –
those were the years of the Glacier and the bar in the Hotel Colón.
    There were society people
who have vanished: Rosa Trènor was one of them,
I met her – not her, of course, but the figure she played: Carmen
    Broto,
who, in those years when it was windy and dark and people used to go
    about in gabardines,
got killed in the vicinity of my grandparents' home and dumped in a
    plot with shattered bottleglass,
Carmen, the blonde who used to pull up at the Liceu in her snazzy
    ship of a car – the years of the maquis,
shootouts on Paral.lel, venom-faced characters,
Sabater's death on blurred display in *El Caso*,
mingled with untold others: those buried alive, the drunken assassins,
    housemaids deflowered – it's nothing special, you see,
on the way from Hospitalet, they waited for him with pistols,
and him or the other one, the invert, and something about an Italian
anarchist, I don't know which. I've mixed all that up:
in those days I didn't read the papers, I was out looking for work,
I had to live, and you used to come with the leather satchel we bought
    you to carry your books,

From *The Mirrors* (Els miralls, 1970)   7

and the pencil case with the coloured pencils, and the things your
    teachers said struck you as normal,
though all that talk about the war a bit less so,
and at home we weren't about to fill you in: we had lived it, that was
    enough.
Anyway, there was no point. Look,
we were happy in '34 and we've even become happy again since,
because people's nature is to be happy: the custom's fading now, but
    you must remember
how you had to close the rolling shutters as a child
to get to sleep on Saint John's Eve, what with the fireworks and the
    people on the rooftops,
and the world seemed to be theirs, these were people who could drink
    and dance and act a fool on the streets in the morning – which we
    either couldn't do
or didn't know how to – but with the barges and the mussel nets and
    the scent of fish and petrol
your mother and me, like young people, even if we had to go home
    early for you, but: shall I tell you, we kissed
under a streetlamp, same as the couples at the fairgrounds
and in the bumper cars?
                                        Everything is so distant to me now,
I no longer remember: nothing, the cup of milk on
the nightstand must have gone cold, I'll have to warm it up
on the burner. This milk has cream in it,
and not the old kind, still, with this taste,
like chemicals, I don't know; the houses aren't the same
nor the records nor the people, not even you – nor the sky,
which turns softer now and pinkish at twilight,
tender and warm like the body of a woman, with muffled brilliance,
and how now, when you walk down the street, you never think
that these agonising lights or my gaze – and yet it is me, look
    close, in the smoke-filled bars, in a red tie
I still remember it, the terraces with dovecotes,
it's not true that we return to the longings of our youth: if it were, I
    would once more yearn
for Mercè, the girl with braids who played with me on the rooftop,

From *The Mirrors* (Els miralls, 1970)

because of the view – nothing special, believe me, a city dusty
    and disgraced – and we rode red bikes
and there was something doing, who knows what, between my
    grandmother and aunt,
even if I never did long for Mercè; for me, women were
something strange, and girls of my age, especially perilous,
I don't know, I was afraid of that world I knew nothing of,
backrooms, hide-and-seek, ironing boards, hallways, braids,
    modest necklines, not a hint of breast, and in the summer
those were the years when they still took me to my grandparents'
    house for the village fair in Gràcia, with the carousels and stalls
    and shooting galleries,
but I couldn't forget that women weren't absent from all that, and
    it unsettled me a bit – it meant leaving my world of Ariosto and
    Salgari and entering the unknown,
which was, once I saw it, all-too known: Ariosto and Salgari both are
    full of the stuff –
and I liked that house of my grandparents', with the curtains and the
    quality of silence and of things come to rest on the eve of the war,
my grandfather's books in the office with the green portfolio – it was
    there that I first read Stendhal:
I learned nothing from him – the radio with its speaker
and the silence, the dominant impression is of silent afternoons, the
    house dormant,
my grandfather seated with a blanket over his legs,
raising his head to say that they always had to throw everything in his
    face
or to remark to me on a passage from *Wuthering Heights*,
and the kitchen with that special scent that excited me, I don't know
    why,
that was my childhood until suddenly it foundered
and one afternoon, when they were taking me to the fair,
I burst into tears in my mother's arms,
and never again did I return, except for visits: then, and in no other
    moment,
I believe my childhood ended.
    You see, it's not so easy

and the years take everything away – this moment in the car windows
   with red lights on the radio recalling Sidney Bechet –
and if I told you how long – though unawares –
   my apprenticeship has been
to grant some cohesion to my dreams,
stinging gold of flesh, nostalgia, memory enkindled,
we've been doomed to live out inexistent years
– what will they say about that? – never has life been so unreal,
everything seems to happen in the past, and is as far away as the past,
the force of endowing life with meaning: might that not be the
primordial function
of art? – those are verses from years ago – and: is the poetic work
an interpretation we propose for what is given? I mean: is it an effort
   at coherence?

From *The Mirrors* (Els miralls, 1970)

Now the Poet Undertakes a Practical Act

Ici commence la grande nuit de mes mots.
ARAGON

Velvet or cotton or silk tempests' gale
The vases Your breasts speak the image mundane
White raven in snow white alders pale plane
Laboratory of opals The water a trail

Pearls from the fish house displayed in the cage
cold of lauds blustering praise songs to night
murmurs of vapor the swords that alight
like the sea recollecting the spaces erased

and the needle that melts in the slivers of nails
water-borne centaur eyelid of my sleep
what country what closed habitations what keep
are the linings of silk marring stars like a veil

In the azurine eyes of the scarecrows are stakes
the rings on the roof clusters bellow up soot
stars in the hollow dead wheat underfoot
the mane of the mare with blue eyes, the pale lake

When the swords bar your body I will not seek for death
bars of darkness bars body body bowed blood in teeth
my stomach a forge my blind eyes fire-wreathed
blood on gums on the palate lungs blow burning breath

Draped in the darkness with arms cut away
in my thorax the organ wheezes its tune
childhood downpours the salt in the wounds
thunder in the garden flood fan water's spray

On the outcrop the lightning bares trophies above
in the mirror white body more iron for the fire
autumnal veneries foxes howling as choir
dry leaves tell the legend the goldenrod glove

From *The Mirrors* (Els miralls, 1970)

Distant

Absent music has devoured
our bodies. The sky obstructing
the sunset. A dark weight, a murmur,
a sunglimmer on bodies. No, autumn's
glow ignites no spring,
nor need the body await it: there is nothing
we do not see. Only this music
burns our bodies like tinder. Silence.
Only a murmur of water. Don't tell me
of the glimmer of bodies, when the woods obscure
the sun, and the sun, with dark fire, obscures
the sun's glimmer. The sword slices
the twilight into halves.
The ideal waters, just the meaning of water,
the idea of water, glow
on field gules of a heraldry absent.
Text written, text negated, canebrake or cinder,
the vast vaporous vessel never finds
its domain, the dead rigging.
Snow-shrouded ship of clouds. What fate?
Without weapons, without buckler or palfrey,
the white horseman of the sky. Blind trees set eyes on
the desolate water, a blind machination of trees.
As the void grips the marrow, clement
in autumn, so the cold grips the eyelids.
Hands of the water, the distance, the dark
emerald green of night in April.
Dry splinters, all those moments,
are they good for something? Dark, the holm oak
abides and awaits, as if the world
were nourished on an instant: of waiting.
Such is the waiting of bodies. Fed by the fire of day
on the obscene hope of flesh,
as though it might be eternal.

From *The Darkening Hour* (Hora Foscant, 1971)

Like, perhaps, the light that burns the forests,
that ignites the branches of iron winter.
Like, perhaps, the dark winter wind
bearing lovers' voices, bodies, useless
trappings of flesh, black professions
of the winter sky, fire of arrows obscure.
Useless profession of the flesh. Falcons'
cries loom over us, like a gravid cloud's rebuke,
cradling us in a destiny of rain. Must the eyes
open fully then, as if to witness
the downfall of the stars? Will they see it,
and the sky choked by the fundament of bodies,
the water of elements and the water of air,
the destiny of light, taking sides
with the shadows, the screen of beings
unfolded, will we see
with new eyes, like a beast sensing rain,
not with the senses, not with hope, not
with the abject and beaten will,
but with the entirety of its being, inexorable
like the night, with the will of the night?
This, perhaps, is waiting. Perhaps the tree
feels it, and knows the sign of the tree
is another, deeper. Thus night,
like a mesh, envelopes the covert
progress of beings, the rubble
of the carnal profession, reddish
strips of sky igniting its theaters.

... that blind fire the lovers ignite.
AUSIAS MARCH

Elegy

To Isabel and Josep Maria Castellet

Perhaps a dark furor of centaurs.
Blue seizure of auras and stars.
Thwarted, furrows beaten, the fall
like a trowel of terminal light.
Stout scepters, tempest, pyrite.
To what fire, dying body, are you in thrall?

A buried cry hushed by the sky above.
Sulfur in the court of the bare, blind grove.
The crag ignited by the setting sun.
Bristly visage of what we lived long ago.
The night espies me with eyes of snow
and I and the black sky are one.

Scowling, my future portends.
No signet seals or ciphers in pen.
No ceremony, no codicil.
At once, the verdict recognised,
They will strip me of my skin and eyes.
Burnt by quicklime, dead as April.

From *Blind Fire* (Foc Cec, 1972–1973)

My passion, my sustenance
red standard of madness,
the warmth of a body of light:
all are rubble, kingdoms razed.
No more do you mourn them in winter days.
Destruction has devolved into rite.

Autumnal, who will return when
the vagabond northeastern wind
prays over the vastness of the oblivion of vice,
bare meadows on the moons,
dark stomach of the nubile dunes,
the bloody scythe wounding the heights?

The nightfall shifts its dark eyelash.
The tremulous wind of the past.
You win what you lose, my heart.
Longing, why now venture forth?
The moon has blood on its horns.
Sylvan, the sky departs.

Winter of crutches. A solitary sough
draws breath from the leaves. The shadow
of the madman grows. In the shroud
of the woods we hang demons. The foul
masks – tongue of gall, petrified scowl –
will utter our truth aloud.

From *Blind Fire* (Foc Cec, 1972–1973)

Vlad Drakul

I

This empire, copious in lindens,
dark monarchy of myrtle, like the shadow
of an eagle, like keys, stone, hinge
of nothingness, when august, the twilight,
draws a dragon over the trees. At night, the clouds
shed their colours: grave-red,
shrine-blue, the green
of gelid eyes. A formless cloud,
immense, body poised, lips breathing
in the tremulous protectorate of velvet.
This breath is no hostage of the dominion
of shadows, no hostage of fingernails
or talons at night, coffer of silver
or cup on the console. Lenten fabrics,
algor and shadow in tatters. Hear
the howls beneath the axle,
see the blood of the owls? Tomorrow,
when the vulture's blind eye cries at noon,
like a triumph of bodies, and in the graves
the snowstorms have shrouded
the spear tips of the crosses, the pale
specter of my memory will utter
vanished shadows of candelabras, wounded clangor
of waters and mirrors, droning copper,
furtive chalice of eyes that close
and lay waste to expired brilliance, the wick
of a breast only shadows shall claim.

From *Blind Fire* (Foc Cec, 1972–1973)

II

Bright like an indigo lance,
the armor of night will discern
below, where the waters advance,
the face of the horse, taciturn
in the mirror with a mournful glance.
The sky draws closed: an urn
cut from impossible glass.

At midnight, alone,
the bodies, wretched dwellers,
do they feel this cold, like stone?
In the sepulchral cellar,
in the marrow of the bones,
flesh torn to tatters,
might Lucifer moan?

With blue sulfur ablaze,
with the blush from soirées,
with my eyes cut away,
with my body enslaved
– ashes, castoff raiments – say:
does it please you to gaze
as this dead vessel strays?
(The snow, the blood become me.)

III

In a guise of silk and dust, autumn
strikes the crumbling shutters, and the old doors
off in eternity – fire suspended in a charred
prison, like the zephyr under the darkened vault,
like the impress of sun, of a scratch in black sky –
speak now of the stiffening of hands, and my mad
summer, and insatiate winter – wolves and waste –
winter, old sparrowhawk of the gypsum fields, mossy
like the touch of bodies, iridescent nacre,
the nude skin, warm and taut, of belly and breast,
cork masks of the old burnt forest,
when the curtains collapse under motionless blue,
and, sterile in the church grounds, the works of iron nails
no more graze the proud golden curtain of evening.

From *Blind Fire* (Foc Cec, 1972–1973)

Blind Fire

For Vicente Aleixandre

Incinerated weight of the ploughshares.
Wheel of the solar Cyclops.
The humming of ravens and roots.
Darker, a sovereign domain.
Swords, their hasps aglimmer.
Rowel spurs pinned to the hands.
Lambs with their throats slit. Slivers.
Sulfur and scree char the plane.
Without scrap metal, rebar, or rings,
who will know you, my body?

And when naked skin seethes
with this breath, and these bindings
of dark silk grade nightward,
will these arms, these eyes
cede the embers, the ash
of forgotten fires in hand baskets
stoked and scattered by the wind?
We travel, arrayed as harlequins,
over the smoldering sands.

Bronze, neglected bells.
Body bound by foot and hand,
wounded and hanged, do you beg
to salvage the light from before,
the doublet of vainglorious silks,
the chambers and instants,
the falcon's wings haughty
over faraway shipwrecks?
Pit graves of sea spray and gold.
Jeweled body, *stil de grain* hand.

From *Blind Fire* (Foc Cec, 1972–1973)

And the stars, now decamping
immobile and sepulchral
through the expiatory dome
that annuls ancient crimes
of elegiac armies, green serpent of day
that snuffs out dark beacons,
the stars cast their light on the madness
of a sunset of kettledrums.
Black cohort, affliction of light,
light glowing black on the outcrops.

The soaring of an eagle,
distaff of a sky perplexed,
can it shatter the darkness,
procurer, black panther, ebony,
of a bed of pleasure, a hollow,
man's succor, derisory
spindle, a body, dreary
dowry, usufruct of shadows
in the abandoned manor?
The moon binds body to body.

The white blaze of hawthorn,
the prone scimitar of night,
the beeches the March light
joins scorching in a sheaf,
the whole of midday disbanded
is a frock torn to tatters:
tunics, a swooning, dear
to the eyes, posthumous, dead
unease. Dark metal, greedy clouds
have conquered the firmament.

From *Blind Fire* (Foc Cec, 1972–1973)

For foxes and ferrets
and the scorpion's claw
have made of the sky
on this bright day their pasture.
Everything is conjury.
I gaze at my frozen hand.
In my heart, countless shadows
come to rest. The horses, the oxen
smell death. Vain fire
consuming an offering impure!

The light vanishes. The tiger's eye,
the panting of the dog, endure.

May

Champs divisés, concédés aux gens d'armes.
NOSTRADAMUS

Now, with the wind and the sulfur of May, the dark
fields divided, fiefs of shadows, men of arms,
regents and kings and chancellors dread,
black falconry. Summer, a dead warrior's arm –
will it light the torches of paroxysmal September?
The space of being in tension,
motive space, the disc of the sun
that reels beyond being, immobile incandescence
assuaging the gesture adjourned and freezing
this world's white flicker, blind clarity,
umbrous ecstasy of galley slaves' eyes.
Thus the eagle finds morning: shadow
is its morning, and the open field of agony and zeal
when depleted, the sky, febrile, and laggard
from its nocturnal past and its rout
in the forests, harvests black scythes and dominion,
and sovereign, bares the brightness of May,
swaddles me in evening blue – fallow frost –
and in silence, the eyes of a polecat
clutch the world. Mad night of May,
night of beatings and chastisements! Green,
the violet sky looms over me. Snow, persecutions.
No clemency, no clamor. The valley obeisant,
laid bare by the light, legacy
and complot of crime. Under the ashen combat,
like lances, the forests sway.

From *Blind Fire* (Foc Cec, 1972–1973)

Solstice

The summer has unearthed the stiff
corpse of spring. Now the eye
will not capture the shadowy waves,
the violet linen in splendor. The straw
ignites, like a torch of lightning,
a tree burnt to a cinder. Vine shoots, sulfurous combat
of roots, murmurs of the earth. Oh heart of man,
winter refuge of warriors! Avid
summers and springs. Febrile
ardor of time scored by my past
to reveal to us the blazing black sun.
Guardians of a baleful game of chess,
of castles and paws, were we lurid
supernumeraries? Kingdom of silence, oaks,
autumn of being. And the metals, bloodless
beneath the stamp, the high dominion. Summer,
meek summer! The frozen sky
is transparency. Smooth, the sea reflects
the diamond, the buried moon,
the fief of the hidden sun. The words
conceal a sunken field, and writing
rends the body of the tiger. Written with fire
and written with light, on the lunar expanse,
the pasture of the dead. The lover descries,
beyond twisted appendages, darkness.
And the roots do not move. Like bodies,
they are nurtured on silence. Their country
of drought and sparks throws
open its eyes. The cry of the crow
bleeds in the violaceous sky. Wood and sapphire:
last glimmer, convulsive, of terrestrial light.

From *Blind Fire* (Foc Cec, 1972–1973)

Vision

Transparent, the shadows
cleave a crystalline void: the pomegranate
of your body, defiant in the kernel
of darkness.
        It is a mental
form that flickers now when, nude,
you burn on behind my closed eyes. I move
like a root through earth's carbon palace,
inverting the destiny of magnetised
branchwork, tense
between air and penumbra: the tree, a being
half buried, in the heart of the whirlwind of signs,
like your body, formed and dissolving,
already, instantaneous, in my eyes.
        Time
is the duration of your nakedness, precipitate
image of dark rotary movement
around the cleft
that gapes, glimmers, and gazes at me in your body's transept.
        Motile confluence:
blades, helices, silence, planetary gale
when your legs open to reveal to me,
like scissors of flame, the moon's remote glaciation
and the pale combustion of the nighttime sky.
Is this me? Dark eyelid,
do you cradle me in your depths, under the shadow you ignite?
To say your body is to say I. To say your body
is to say the unsaid. Your body ever says
the unsaid. Constant, it speaks it
with its lingering crackle of singular fruit,
of fruit I think and say and it dazzles me:
in the light, it is light, it is the instant held fast,
reverberation mingled with matter,
vision of the concept, body rendered *idée fixe*

          Three Poems (Tres poemes, 1974)

that will not vacate my retina, that lingers
like the impress of scorched sun.
In two times distinct,
the word and the body, the pupil
and the nakedness that creates it.
                                    Expanse of shadows,
form over form,
instants, perceptions, shards of sound
shaved from the last sound, from the muffled gyration
of lovers bound to a single quadriga
over the oceanic glowering of the firmament.
                    Hands and lips,
and still more, respirations,
breath, like agate, mingled with your breath
exhaling splendor, and now I round
the crested swellings, your bright buttocks,
breach your luminous temple, and espy
in the depths the fiery eye that awaits me,
the nocturnal ruby throbbing like a cyclone
just as, beneath the black flash of your pubis
the marine transparency of your grotto
called to me before: you are one, with
two eyes, two cenotes, two solar abysses.
Blason and vision, ceremony
mounted amid a combat of archangels on high:
fallen curtains, pillaged gold, abysses,
time's theater. To make the instant endless,
is that to make the body endless? The light of the body,
will it make us endless? I no longer see it: I erase
the gaze with the gaze. Time
sees itself in this body
and seeing itself, is annulled. Evening
flashes: it is a mirror, and the waves
in the depths of the mirror. The body navigates
in a crystal of iridescent light.
Possession and dispossession. Ephemeral
trophies of night, armaments of sun

and fog, where are we? What space shrouds us,
in what dark glass gleams our desire?
The appearance is the instant. Of death, I know
nothing but the iron escutcheons of masked time.
Only once does it show its face,
then we die from a fulminant kiss. The red
sky mimics the red waters of sunset:
your body mimics nothing. Silence, bronze,
suspended explosion, incandescences,
nudity denying the night, blackening snow,
hostage to this bedroom. Unique, the instant
is past and is present, and now I remember
that now I disrobe you, fulgurant, and now
I was embracing you, and now I see you, already seen,
beneath the deceptive makeup of the vacated sky,
and your body, so uncertain, is the singular certainty:
your body is certainty made splendor.

Three Poems (Tres poemes, 1974)

Unity

To María José and Octavio Paz

Dictated by twilight,
dictated by dark air, the circle opens
and within it, we abide: transitions,
intermediate space. Not the place
of revelation, but the place
of reencounter. The rapier
that bisects the sun.
                      From eye to gaze,
permanent brightness, ambit of sound,
bell that embraces terrestrial vision
as the inexorable eye of floral form
fixes the flame of a garnet. This eye,
does it see my eye? The eye that now sees me
is a mirror of fire. With the sound of rotation,
the axis of night. Dismasted,
darkness collapses, and tentatively,
sun makes the acquaintance of night.

Night in April

Mind blank, with the sky blue clarity
of an old zodiac aglow: empty vault,
blue and compact, pellucid form
sheltered in form. Thus I find myself,
on the prowl for a street. It isn't here, it never was:
it exists in levitation, now,
for the mind devises it. Surly siege,
plaint of visible and invisible: flame
and consummation. Contours, immobile
crystallising stone. Tonight,
a storm of eyes, a storm a word designates
without saying it entirely, like the reflection
of a pearl in shadows. Now the fingers
burn with the clarity of a word. The sun?
The nocturnal solar body, in shards, tumbles
downsky, downskin. Not even tactility
can arrest its fall. Blazing
and puissant. By morning, they water
the streets, and a silence bare of claxons
in the damp passages discloses an empire
where skin answers skin, where the knot
ties and unties itself. Orion's torches
look on the interlaced bodies. Astral
stage of curtained depths
over sonorous splendor. You utter
one word, the word of touch, the sun
my hands grasp, the sun made body,
the tactile quality of the word. And tactile, inviolate,
the stars, carriage skidding
into the depths of grey glass and reflected
in your luxury, glow of buttocks and back,
the fixed, igneous orb: the verso
lays bare the dark thunder of the mons veneris.
Two shadows shine when the firmament

Three Poems (Tres poemes, 1974)

shifts the galleys and oars, and now I hear
the lap of waves, the splash of breasts and stomach
copied by the night. The cosmic room
is the room of the body, nor does white
mingle high clouds with the green of foam:
it delegates everything, it conveys everything. They quake,
in hopes of receiving a name, the creations
of the darkness, the portrait of the two bodies'
pincers, the sky's blanket, rotating
horoscope. Meaning? Everything is doubled now:
words and beings and darkness.
But listen: further off, from corners
and lampposts of night, unmurmuring,
unknown negative of magnesium,
I come, my face comes, and that face
becomes my face again, as if they stamped out
my eyes, my lips, with a dye, everything,
in the toilsome reunion with this other – a trace
made with charcoal – whom I don't know, who
seizes the ice, who melts and freezes me.
This is the adversary, the thing I feel,
derisory and sovereign, eye or scorpion,
the name of the animal, the erstwhile domain.
Does love call for it? When tooth and nail
prowl the skin's blue perimeter,
when the appendages clench, does certainty
emerge from a remoter depth? Bent, the lovers
plunge, like mineral forms
thrown off by the night that the world burns to ash.

Deserted Space

I

Now I see from afar those bodies
all passing, as if spurned by the light of cruel
spring: vital, tense, like metal
mesh, today is destitute of volumes: it opens
and closes, never dilating, stiff, mineral, all dust
and dry copper on the fingers, without sounds, without images,
suspended time of the future.
                    I saw them formerly,
and being sacred, they were one to me, or failed
to take on bodily forms: intangible
as fancies, inventions
or fears of desire: we may meet
beneath a sky of black branches, atremble,
parched slivers of of mica and slate,
this light of loam, of stagnant water, a being
of lichen and ivy, vegetal and putrid,
an emanation from the rarefied space
where the tree lives the cycles of power, time
of kindling and time corroded, when covert, luxuriant,
the fungus pours forth its greenish gold,
body of damp grass, gleaming ring, unmoved,
copper coin in the dead well that remains
a mesmeric corpse of lighting.
                    Thus, parched,
the inverse of day vibrates, refracting these bodies,
and this sky as nude as a stalk of water
and this crystalline clarity of snow
know the voices of the grub and the grass of the snail and the sermon
    of the toad and the beetle that lives from excreta and languishment
    of hyacinth and opal.
What does desire know of this? Everything, perhaps,
obscurely, as when, on the luminous

planet of skin, it calls haltingly
the seclusions of an armpit by name, the sour
and sumptuous fire of the black pomegranate, floral juices of the pubis
and sand of the vegetal and bosky belly.
Haltingly, it recognises this body is identical
to the kingdom of grass. It falls, like sulfur,
the yellow veil of this dreaded day. Parched,
the fissures of clouds trace signs in the sky, empty pond, cold silver
    misted over
with the breath of plants, drunken, sulfurous,
at the hour when bodies recollect a fate
that seizes them, image of tainted waters
and withered sand.
                A glass goblet,
imperial, aquatic, refractant
movements, gestures, eyes, protracted,
yes, everything said in a low voice.
                'Before, I used to sit
and watch them from the distance. I couldn't bring my hand
to them without shattering their cohesion, their
material weight, as when we touch a reflection in water. They
    resembled
me and were not me. They
told me a story, one I might
I have some role in. And now
they dissolve.'
            A sun
in liquefaction, sun of sunsets and mist,
half-frozen, flaying the living skin of night.
Sun of diviners wending their way with lamps lit
with spleen oil and oil of the blood of calves: lavender
and rosemary, devil's snare or mole grass
that blinds us to witness a deeper sun, and the gnashing of teeth
and the gleam of the mole that gnaws at the sun in the depths of the
    eyes.
        The wheel
must bear away the terrace, too, the paths,

the folding chairs, the coloured awning,
the streets beneath the clarion downpour of that summer,
slipping past, and we laughed, the blue handle of an umbrella, and the
    eyelash
trembled like a soundless throb, and now hands meet
and eyes meet eyes.
               This too
the wheel must bear away. I free words
resonant of sabots and wet wood.

II

The live vegetation of the trunk,
when the boy, with eyes like a seer, used to swim in the liquid clarities
    of the closet,
faces, grotesques, eyes making flickers,
beards gold and aqueous, oils
embalming a dry skeleton,
a body shriveled at the end the hallways,
the mask, burnt with acid, of fear,
the majesty of an igneous and fuliginous world, aquarium of red
    clouds going dark,
ever at the edge of collapsing into absence.
                     And the wood,
which creaks secretly and shifts, hearkening
a sound of sabots, haughty touch of plumage and shimmers of *eau de
    vie*,
the wood, exiled to a country of cork,
lapped by waters, by leopards of sun,
nude and refulgent, burns in the storehouse in the port, prodded by
    candles,
statuary, leprous, with marble froth,
with frost of scintillant salt and sickly green.
Men of corroded and verdigris bronze
up the quay, with dark leathern visors, pale and vague
under the iron claw and the shadow of the outspread wings of the
    cranes.

                      From *Deserted Space* (L'espai desert, 1976)

Up the quay, in silence, with the glimmer of the hooks,
dusty, in a diafilm frame,
stationary, instant, beneath a light of magnesium,
brandishing rifles and harpoons.
                              The myths
of adolescent time, the knife of Theseus
that would do justice at last, partition
between today and the time that inaugurates another time.
The years of abjection, time of birds of prey and bloodhounds stalking
    Catalonia,
time of tusks, time of the serpent's stutters and the stammering of the
    rapinous rattler,
time of the buffalo's bellow, time of homage to the fatuous crab and
    the murderous hedgehog,
the years of our humiliation, the empire of the lash,
and the sudden mythic space, when, glimmering, we would see,
after men with beaks of black vultures and men with heads of spiders
    and men with heads of polecats and scorpions,
instated in a new time,
men with faces of men.
                              This grisaille
of sirens, of smoke and barges,
of chimney stacks black and tainted with soot,
the wall of bricks, the empty street with swatches of tar,
the one thing visible
to the eyes of a face drawn in dust on blind glass.
Dust eyes, dust features, echoed
in a luster that erases the gaze
of this face in the glass, seeing my face, assaulted by the blue
and a maritime quiver of clouds.

III

The cadaverous circle of the family,
with sordid oily blotches, like a sprinkling of dandruff,
faces withered, eyes cold in bare sockets in the golden glow,

nails tinged with blue that feel
for smoke and turpentine, feel for the bedcovers, eyes fixed, keys
    tucked away,
eyes vacant and faces corroded by bleach,
the skin of the air is the skin of *acidum salis*,
the skin like blue tracing paper, dry paper, eyes decals,
one colour, and the rigid head, with the lacquer that creaks when it
    shifts
(two layers of pigment, brushed on, to highlight the eyes, and a single
    swatch of rouge
on the forehead).
                    Many nights
having dined, we had to wind them back up:
to begin, we grease the hinges and the pistons,
straightened a skewed head, knocked dust from their garments,
and the family set to work.
                    A touch of red,
like tomato, on the cheeks, denoted
chastity; panting prattle gave shape to
the children's obedience; and a hook
for a hand stood for conjugal love.
                    On the streets,
driving candy-painted cars, the wolf pack, in tailcoats,
hordes of people who live for the night,
vixens, wild dogs, the python, the bear
supping blood and eating viscera on the bartops in bars.
Hair parted, slicked back, eyes bruised in deep sockets,
a crescent of red under corneal blue,
the pupil burned down to absolute white,
white blazers, striped trousers – black, yellow, pearl grey – under
    Chinese lanterns,
with the feel and the crackle of paper, trimmed with scissors,
flapping their hands and their arms, with bolo ties and panama hats,
as I play the first notes of the ballad of nacre
on a barrel organ or a music box covered in cracks.
                    Pearls, like an arcane
    pounding of ivory,

From *Deserted Space* (L'espai desert, 1976)

on the tie, and pearls on the somber copper of the body.
                                        Mad priestess,
black tigress, fulminant flesh, radiant
coal and rubies, vegetal and carnivorous bonfire,
in a gasping of green vines,
with a dark and sour scent of saffron!
Priestess of velvet and iron,
spilling the algoid blackness of your belly
over my face submerged in the fierce white waves, petrified,
of your body's twin columns, furnace of a nocturnal sun with black
    petals.

V

I associate rainfall with the dead. It comes slow,
with spikenards and tubers, with the chill of the lilies
and pasty clods of worked soil,
with the venation of leaves, with shadows,
with quail flight and owls' cries.
Earthward, timeward, in the heart of the loam,
who knows of them? They wait, for such is the cycle
of fertility. The buried axe
shines with silver more alive, with mineral fire.
And this is the law. The rain rinses furrows
from wheels in the soil, from scores of carriages past,
from prints of men's feet and horse's hooves. A grey and liquid film,
stifled brilliance, as of dark and opaque steel
over the sodden soil. Don't you hear those voices,
girls' laughter at midday in August?
Don't you see this red blouse? Like a root,
a hand still digs the damp soil, withered
fingers with crooked claws, arid, of sack paper
and skin. No, the rain doesn't reach
this kingdom. It falls slow, comes
devoutly to greet the olive tree's trunk
polishes the cuspidate grain of the stone,

tames the boggy waters of the lake,
enraged with smoke, floods the den
of the vixen, the rabbit's warren, the nightingale's nest.
But it fails to penetrate the saturated mud,
the mass of porous humility,
of patience, of light, to reach the darkest demesne,
land of rancor and dessication of the dead,
who go on outstretching their hostile hands, ferrous,
with festering teeth and erect sex, trembling,
mummified, and scrape the skin
with a fervor of nails and dust. Will they possess us
or do they merely demand to return?
Demand vexation and tremors and pain?
Do they demand uncertainty, perhaps,
for their days, to feel the tumult of desire,
the hammer blow of panic, the rage
for domination, the dread of defeat?
Do they dare to long to live again?
As the root lives, the tuber, the grass,
can these men not live again, too,
confided to fate? Will they not concede to the cycle
of fecund time and of the time of return to the earth?
For all the pain borne before,
for the fleeting ardor of all these bodies,
for the memories quickened by this shower of light
and this savor of newly damp earth,
for the quaking of air when the rain
has ceased not long ago, and a bird takes flight
in a limpid silence, and for the colour
of this bird, inconclusive in the blue, which warbles
when the sky has brightened, for the suffering
we recollect, for the loves from before,
and humiliated innocence,
and desires unconfessed,
for all this – will we never have a word?
The rain seeps into the straw lofts of the old plantations,
rots the wood, cuts channels through the tillage

From *Deserted Space* (L'espai desert, 1976)

and nurtures the narcissus. Ashen is its colour,
which on the windows is the colour of memory.
There is only one time. Time of man
and time of beast, time of plant
and time of stone, are one. The falcon
that sinks from the heights
knows its fate, like the stone in the depths of the cistern
seeing its fate in a flicker of water.
They see it of a sudden, it annuls
and clasps them, they attain splendor: attain
the fulguration of being. And thus they come
to be what they are. Faithful, silent,
like the sunburnt Kermes oak, they say yes,
they know it is yes, that this image
– glint of dead water, or abode of shadows
in the heart of the brush land at eventide –
is what they are, it beseeches them to die there,
and this death is a having lived,
not an interruption or deferment.
They say yes, with the sense that they need regret
nothing, await nothing, that nothing is shorn
for everything already was:
they ever lived in the time of the inland of shadows,
the time of dead water in the depths of the well.
When we pass, by night, by the rustle
of wind fanning the leaves of the poplars,
or gather resplendence in clusters
in the lambent glory of noon,
or close, halfway, the shutters – the sun
a hammer on the empty streets – and a body
breathes warm on us, redolent of lemons,
or when we see a yellow stone in the forest
or hear a crackle of water and branches,
do we know everything will be this single instant?
Do we hope for anything more? Amnesiac,
dispossessed, time's mirror no more dazzles us,
its feldspar reflections no longer cloud our eyes.

I am my yesterday, and feel the immanence
of the future throb in each gladiola.
It doesn't espy us behind each instant: it is each instant.
It does not sport the dark face of our unease,
nor must we ask it for pity. Did we not always have the sense
that we were bearing it? Desire,
you dark slave in the mask of a prince,
and passion, you princess pale and blind,
who laugh attired in the brilliance of lilies,
do you not sense that your hour is the instant?
We do not win, we do not lose. The dead
abide in the eternal nocturne of fog,
the instance that is all time: the time of desire
and passion, the time of memory
and the time of sleep. The vapor of the brume
and a smoke cloud as of green wood
point to the location of our dreams: far off,
like the lighting on a summer night.

VIII

With firm steps, thundering through plantations and forests,
the bogeyman comes up the road.
                              If you tell me
I didn't live all these years, that time
is the glow of this white pile of bones,
this revel of white on the sand flats,
that I will have lived nothing, in a clarity
of diamond and glass, if you tell me that in the persistent
glow of the paralyzed twilight of fire
I am the same person who heard those steps
in the empty attic of that winter night,
if you tell me he is coming now, that already the nursemaid
is shutting the door, and I arrive from the garden
when a sooty cloud chars the sky
and we feel the coming rain, the drum blow

From *Deserted Space* (L'espai desert, 1976)

of thunder on the walls of the celestial cave,
and I sense how a darkness dangling in the air
– as if everything were smothered by a bindlecloth –
how the luster, strangled by a black bandana
and the puncheon of the rain in my eyes from before
tell me: those steps are approaching, like a shadow
I now see, the lilaceous eyes of a death
on legs, the bluish beard, the grating
laughter of the sparrowhawk, the trepidation
of paths and forests trod by talons
the glow of rotten teeth, the gallows,
the rope of the hanged man furrowing my throat,
and if I am the one who is now screaming,
if now I see the reddish tongue,
the frozen rictus and the hanged man's empty eyes,
if now, in the windows of the kitchen, darkened
by a stormy sky, I see his talons dancing
like a doll, those talons now wending their way,
pounding through the forest as he shoulders his sack
because I did not live all those years: the door swings
open, and the sky on the tiles
leaves a gleam of incandescent bronze, and taut,
the air feels in the garden's foliage that apprehension
that I feel, a pounding in my chest, because he is here,
he is walking in the attic, he steps through the storm door
and now calls at the door with his iron hand,
in my chest, an iron hand grasps me,
at the open door of my chest, like the sky
stifled by the light of the tempestuous wind,
turbid with leaves intermingled with mud,
a dark wind in the pond, black with glimmers
under the dread of the sky in my open eyes,
and if you tell me that this is all that I've lived,
the moment of fear, a voyage through closed rooms
with weighty locks, hiding my face,
with wheezes, under the cushion, my heart
pounding to the rhythm of the steps in the attic,

From *Deserted Space* (L'espai desert, 1976)

resounding on the dark path of birds and pine brakes,
deafening, through the walls of the old plantations,
and the breadth of a step is the breadth of thunder,
and if you tell me I am he, holed up
in the bedroom, afraid of the basins
and the instruments of night, the sign of the cross,
the char of sparks at nightfall,
the fear of the lizards when lightning pursues them,
and if you tell me I've lived nothing, because I am bound,
hanging head-down, to the darkness of beams,
and if you tell me the moment of nocturnal fears,
the moment of waiting for the pitchforks to wound,
the moment of waiting till they thrash me like wheat,
hunched under the hoarfrost of shadows and sheets,
if you tell me all that is the time I am living, because I wake
and those deafening steps advance in the silence
and the house is the nocturnal house of panic,
manse of winter and rust, of windstorms
open to the sanguineous light of the paths,
and these steps are mine, and I walk through the forest,
clutching the rope draped around my bruised neck,
and I extinguish the darkness with my steps,
and I guard the darkness in my badly darned sack,
and when the rain comes, I will see the face
that awaits me, white and earthen, my face
in this bed where I lie, where I open my eyes in the morning
and live in a crepuscule of the mind, a livid light
of hanged men, where the bogeyman stalks, a man
with my face, with a landscape in his eyes,
a landscape of forests, of vacant plantations,
all the fear in the world lived in an instant,
the anguish of those rainy afternoons bearing down on my chest,
the anguish of breathless light, the wind
that rends my chest, and with my nails I scratch
the sheets, expecting the face of a dead man,
a yellow unreal, because all too real,
the intensity of inner time that I live,

From *Deserted Space* (L'espai desert, 1976)

and if you tell me words that do not sound, opaque,
and if he buries our face in a black bag, a dark
scrap of sackcloth, coarse on the skin,
and the words sound like a babbling of blisters,
like bubbles of mud burst and abandoned,
now I listen, and I know that I rise, and, in the darkness,
I still hear those steps, I live in that night.

IX

Radiances.
            Radiances in the eyes.
                        Shades of radiance.
Orange and black. No: blue, carmine.
Yellow splendor. Like eyes. A yellow mask.
Red on closed eyes. Black. A red night.
The sun, like a wheel. The millstone.
Radiances. The white poplar. The white cry. The white sun. With all
    this white,
I can't see it. A white flame. Colour. Vanished.
A white that burns. The ignited circle of white.
The eye. Black. Radiances. The black cockerel. The red peacock.
The earth masked in yellow. The radiance of black.
The vanishment of black. I move toward yellow. Yellow fire.
The yellow vanishment of broom. The sun
like a black stone. The eye. The mill of radiances.
The wheel of radiances is a white sun. The cry
of the red cockerel. The black pearl. The peacock is the center
of the wheel. The mill of brightness. The wheel
of the sun. Yellow. White. A furnace in the eyes.
    Red.
The peacock in the retina. Green. The darkness of green.
Radiances. Green is black. Blue is white. Vanishment.
The eye sees black. White is green. I see a mill.
Toward black. Burning. Vanished. Toward white.
A red cockerel. Eyes. Radiances in eyes. Black.

From *Deserted Space* (L'espai desert, 1976)   41

X

The hollow of being. Ever the same
words, with the clang of false metal
or straw fires, with the feigned luster
of trinkets, white and spectral,
as though, once more, the scene filmed before
were repeated, these gaslit
streets, a postcard of London
at night, an enigma, all of it,
like your belly, the black roots
of the *mons veneris*, cavern of lighting
leaving a savor of sulfur on our lips,
fish of flame in a night of foam.
We will meet each other in the hollow of being,
the fundament of the world of matter,
an absolute space, the fathoms
of the tenebres, when the optic nerve
knows no silence, the blue of vibrations.
The sparkling night burns our eyes.
With the cinders fall the images of time.
This world without brilliance, without touch, trembles not,
matte air and dust from charcoal.
A dark paper blows through the mineral space.
Not the wind nor the words nor the light
in this hollow, not the darkness: the absence
of sensory data, as if the roof
were thrown open to the cold, and space to space.
Space devours space and collapses it:
the hollow of being opens to vacancy.
Pure exhalation, exhaling space
that cleanses the senses, the nude grotto,
the fathomage of exhalation.
We speak the hollow, speak the vacant place of being.
A whitish water, swallowed by smoke.
We will return to the night, to the smudged postcard
with leaden colours of a livid dawn,

From *Deserted Space* (L'espai desert, 1976)

to the swatches of sun, cold in a deaf clarity
to the waters of the river, the bridges of darkness,
the bell of molten light of autumn,
these streets lived before, in a vaporous
scene, like a double of our lived time,
and we will see again that green glove of silk
on the gold of the door of the dead carriage,
the pearls in the turban of the goddess
the polished glimmers of the night at the hotels.
It is a lithograph
on paper that crumbles, slow
like leaves descending in a dream.
There is no transition: we open our eyes
in the dark in the bedroom. The wings
of birds beat in the blackness. Is it now
that we've begun to dream? The visible world grows,
intuited in the light of imaginary time.
Like panting in a darkened room,
living in the space of the hollow of being, living
left nothing but a throb, with a momentary sun
in the pupil's depth, a blind sun that doesn't burn,
a sphere of ice in the bedroom.
Listening to the nothingness, inhaling an absence
of air in a caisson, in a barometric
zero, the hibernal void,
in non-time and non-space, the void
that tears at my lungs when I breathe
until I feel breathed in by the void,
the non-space that respires me, the formidable
lungs, and I am the breathing,
the breath of non-space, when it inhales
and exhales, when it blows me into an enclosure,
here, in the dark bedroom, in the convex sky
that flees the light, and I feel the lungs
of the night inhale me in a bedroom,
I feel the pounding, I am the pounding, the sky
that pounds, the light that has held its breath,

to leave a luminosity stripped of space,
to strip space of luminosity,
to see the depths of the hollow of being,
to see space without brightness or darkness,
to see space where there is no space,
to see the space that is all space.

From *Deserted Space* (L'espai desert, 1976)

Light of Velintonia

For Vicente Aleixandre

Present in the clarity suspended, this garden
is time's habitation.
                    Shoot of tenebrescence
fundament of the uninhabited sky,
puissance, pulsions that germinate and explode
in the flora of the air.
                    Time is invisible
like the light of the garden: the garden is visible
behind the glass, not the image of the garden
in the successive light of temporality.
But another garden is visible as well: not a real place
that was, nor a place that existed in the mind,
not the succession of time in a single place,
but the persistence of atemporal time.
Arrect in an invisible setting, the garden
makes visible the light.
                    If the voice designates
the clarity of this tree, if on the gate hands
enter the light of levitant place,
if we step into the center of an instantaneous whirlwind,
we are, without light or time, in invisibility.
The word of a man makes visible the real:
in the light, we may see the garden as garden.

Land of Antoni Tàpies

The winter wears the colour of marble dust.
A forge of green clarities seethes
under the visible light of the branches, so clear
because so nude, enclosure of fires in April.
We belong in a land throbbing with water and grass,
a trickling of mists in the gorge of the sky.
Marble dust, rock, cardboard, and scrap metal
have greeted the arrival of the seasons,
heritage of time that envelopes man,
ceremonial gold and tremulous green,
nocturnal blue, the blue seen by closed eyes
in the ring of dark fog that irradiates appearances.
We belong in this land, this legacy, exemplar
of the glow of the poplars and the nude window
that sees the utter transparency of the void.
A land to return to, even deeper
than we seek, even deeper
than we might manage to dream:
a country where darkness was conciliation
of space and of man, like the root of space
piercing the subsoil, like the soot of the subsoil
piercing the black mines of the firmament.
To return there is to return to the land where instants
neither die nor are born: present, irreducible,
repudiating memory, they are nothing beyond awareness.
Like the hand, like the body, like the fever-racked mind,
all being now ceases to mar its surroundings.
Now the time has come to wait and to greet,
time of tools flung into the water of the gulfs,
navigation of ruins, monastery
of sheets and moss, country of blood.
Time of men who have found suddenly a domain:
the pure clarity of knowing that they live.

Two Homages (Dos homenatjes, 1978)

Apparitions

I

Dreaming doesn't always have colour or movement:
at times, it is a state. And my dream last night
was silent and green like water,
and like water it was dark, perhaps with the mere trace
of some living thing gliding beneath the sky.
But a mental sky, as when eyes see
with a vision of eyes turned inward:
not sensory vision, nor the recollection
of sensory vision; not the tremulous
colour of a cloud bleeding out,
but that which, red, like an echo of light,
breathes again when the western wind subsides.
The dream of last night was a state: not the center,
but the shore, the outskirts of the world.
Before objects, as though sustaining the object;
before me, before that instant
in which I will say: 'I am I', and it will still be a dream,
but, while dreaming, with the feeling that, when opening my eyes,
if I remember it, I will know that already I was someone.
Nothing could jolt me or matter to me yet
because I was not yet a being: I was only
a state, a waiting. At times comes obliquely
a very fine rain, on the first nights
of a winter too long delayed. It is cool already
and the sky is a purple-darkened beacon,
and these half-empty streets seem from another time.
It rained like this, dulcet rivulet
with that dead point of shop windows,
half-blurred by the waters of yesterday's cities.
This is what I wanted to say: a state of this kind,
unsure if it is lived or remembered –
the very moment we find ourselves in –

without impulse toward anywhere, without feeling
the need to leave anything behind, or that anything belongs to us.
Neither relinquishing nor holding. I was
a thing of which I could not say that it had a name at all.
Poised to pounce, awaiting the bestowal of identity:
the state of flowing water, or of water still,
identical to metal that will strike it all at once.
Brilliance of water mixed with brilliance of metal:
metal doubled in my eyes, made a lone metal of water,
the metal of the mind and of the senses,
one light, freed from being light,
an idea of light. Because the theme of the dream
is the idea of the I. Confusedly, I felt
that in that stunted greenish splendor
I was projecting acts, or the shadow of what I am.

II

If the sky cries to you, if you hear the sky cry to you
with a cry from the abyss, to suck you
upward, downward, where the mane
of the astral snow goes dark
or the squamous iciness of night,
or if, even louder, you yourself cry
and cannot cease to hear, with a voice as hoarse
as in the pallid ear of a deaf man,
or insidious and naked like water
that wounds the moon with an axe-like splendor:
if you cry toward the center of yourself, if you feel
that all that crying is finding a center
and the knot of light that you are appears to you;
if, within you, you are cried to, will you see,
perhaps, when you rise, that dream I dreamt last night?
See is not quite the right word: I didn't see it,
rather I myself was my dream.
Not that I saw myself, but rather

From *Apparitions* (Aparicions, 1980)

there was something and it was I.
The theme of appearances
is the theme of the self. But this time
I saw no concrete identity:
no image appeared to me.
I didn't unfold, didn't gaze. It was
a null state, the negative of living,
the silence of the river divested of water,
the clarity of a sky bereft of blue
and yet sky: an invisible glimmer,
sensed as a void of visibility.
Such is the bed of a river: soil, rock, repose
of the devastated drought, branch, green rancor
that abandoned the vegetal world, damp
drunk down by the wasteland. The light glances
and, look, all is rock and hunger and dust:
yet the water lives there. It is a region of absence
violent like the sun, which doesn't flow,
but instead is immobile. It is an iron enchased,
the water now free from being water, weighing
on the riverbed. Like the murmur water
makes when not running in the bed of the dry river.

III

Over the tracks the oxen came dark
when I stopped to listen. The luminous
letters and liquids of the gas station
and the weak raking of the crickets. Oil
was poured into the night.
                             The world wasn't there,
and it was there more than ever: pricking the ears, a
faraway hunter's horn.
                             I have known the synthetic
night, prison of bubbling plastics,
frozen and pestilent brilliance that breathes
to stifle my chest. Above all, the silence

is defined in terms of natural night:
night of earth before man, night
of man before being. To breathe, bit by bit,
as if we weren't breathing, or as if breathing
was already the whole of life, as if a whole life
did not suffice to feel respiration.
To feel the respiration of the world? Yes, at times,
up on a hillock, the idea of dominion, perhaps
of a peace that reconciles the world
with its appearance. From inside to out,
a path that divides what it unites: the two provinces
of what is and what is seen. We hear a pounding
like the faraway machinery of night:
it never ceases. To go deaf, to leap
past this lone murmur,
like nude prey in the fauces of the void,
the molars of the snorting and shifting darkness.
Not swallowed: at a distance, as though suspended, without center,
to leap past the center, to see the world respire.

VIII

Acorn, honeysuckle,
powerful citron,
Peiking lilac,
the violent splendor of the sparrows in summer,
the rosebush under the sun,
the pomegranates like red fog,
reverberation of the eye,
the church of green apples,
colour of canes blown by wind,
word of mud and marsh,
carob tree in flames,
the marigold, the begonia,
the carnation of whitest light,
the blackberry,

From *Apparitions* (Aparicions, 1980)

parliament of river and moss,
the breath of the plant when it speaks,
treading a silence made of vibrations,
when we walk through the water,
when we are wind,
when the brightness prods and transfigure us,
dissolved in a carmine of clouds,
the lances level all of it:
the path, the pickets,
the fruit,
the blue pear at nightfall,
with the blue of iridescent sky,
the darkened, tragic ivy,
the corruption of the pepper,
the twilights like water,
the lances level all of it, the flattened
paths make a creaking like wheels
of dead carriages, of wood and carcasses,
scent of sandalwood rotting,
lividity of trees besieged,
lances of light and of gold,
pillage of peapods and Japanese medlars,
brilliance of buckshot and old shotguns,
the hunting pavilion,
the dark gazebo,
the body of this woman is an inferno of silk,
moist like burnt leaves
in a November forest, when the light
has the colour and savor of ash,
rivulets of resin and juice from the bark,
the taste of roots and bruised fruit,
the taste of a woman's urine, pearling and warm
like the ambarine night, taste of summer and memory
when the lances labor on the stubble of winter.

Yesterday, I saw an apparition:
beneath the colonnade, at night, the queen of the harvest

and of the fruit trees, queen of gifts
and offerings. When the year turns
these vapors make their way,
when the harvest overflows like a river of corn
and fructescent blood,
when the sickle slices the air, naked as a ring,
the queen comes
from the fires of the night and the corners,
queen of garlands and sap,
of flourishing and fruiting,
the queen nude like a fatuous fire
and draped in the cape of the imperial forest,
queen of water and trunk,
summoned to the hearth with charcoal and embers,
who, when it darkens, is called to the circle,
by those who are now but a voice in the night.
Queen of time and of environs,
blazing scratch
on the live skin of clarity,
queen of the gold on the nuptials of the trees,
of the light that batters the cavern,
queen of the canticle intoned by the willows,
queen of the seed that empties light,
of the olive and the voices of grape clusters,
queen of the brilliance of the belfry
heard in the depths of the chest, like the clang of handbell
of very clear and very white sound that we recall
when dreams spill over us glasses of darkness.

It is this clang, so pallid
it is not even a clang,
soft as the skin of a magnolia,
this shaded transparency,
that rings in the far away like the shadow of a garden,
like what we remember after living,
this clangor that brightens,
that makes us more luminous,

From *Apparitions* (Aparicions, 1980)

clang of darkness and seasons,
which perhaps we will be, clang of water blue and dead,
clang of women's eyes when they see morning,
sweet like an almond in the blackness,
it is this clang, the feel of your stomach on my lips, warm
as the scent of cinnamon inhaled in the night,
it is this clang, the voice of the world and the harvests,
the baskets of light of summer and winter,
the lead of autumn, the white of spring,
the brambles, the honey,
the fig trees in flower,
this clang that hears us whenever we hear it,
like our past or like the earth,
that will leave us the world full of forests,
of apparitions and transparencies,
the clang of this life that trembles,
the dark flame we bear in our breast,
the one gift this life grants us: pallid
and friable as it is, we call it love.

From *Apparitions* (Aparicions, 1980) 53

Time

Neither sterile pity nor dour penitence:
to know that we are this. Thus the hawthorn accepts decease
and knows it is hawthorn still beneath the nude wind hissing in the
    darkness,
so soft, black, and rigid we fail to hear it pass when it shifts the cane
    brakes.

As an Epilogue (Com un epíleg, 1980)

Winter

Precise as hoarfrost, dour night.
Trees: allegories on the road.
This silence prods us amid clotted light.
The whole of my being erodes.

Poetic Art

More than bestowal of synthesis:
to see in the light the transit of the light.

Sculpture

The marble is violent in the brittle air.
In mute combustion, a buried fire blows:
spirit splitting stone. So, a tree standing bare
melts into shadows and glows.

Fate

Already, night is falling. Dark covers the tracks of the quail.
Like man. Winter: a temple of water and hail.
Cries, cries high in the dogged sky, nude husk!
The light, purblind saturnia, falling brusque
to its death in our bed will end its travail.

As an Epilogue (Com un epíleg, 1980)

Memories

Immemoriality. And is memory
this white that now cleanses our eyes?
Of the moon's splendor, of the autumn of glory,
of the forest in apotheosis, red and transitory,
will we have – like a book burnt – mere traces of leaves?

Vigil

Above the fragility
of the lunatic soul
the gods grant surety
of the night sky unscrolled.

A surfeit of nectar
on our lips turns sour.
Ferocity: specters.
The light will cower.

Turbid from excess of life,
I enter the shadows' lair.
Nocturnal, alone, and free of strife,
all luminosity, the air!

As an Epilogue (Com un epíleg, 1980)

Landscape

We think only of this water that lies dead.
Only of rocks and the avid marsh.
Null, absolute, the circle of silence is a ring of iron harsh.
Perhaps beyond the night throbs a firmament of lead.

Death

In the garden, like a flame,
a thirst higher, more pure
than the white light that tortures
my nuptials with the day.

As at night, when you hear
the trot of a cavalcade,
and, dark, the hooves' cannonade
draws sparks as the road wends near.

Thus, like the descent of time
into obscurity sublime
from the recesses of the blue abyss:

the splendor, inviolate, bare,
of being nothing more than bliss,
like a forest amid the foreday's glare!

As an Epilogue (Com un epíleg, 1980)

Philistines

And so they cannot write poems. It's enough that they shatter
  stoneware,
that they clatter and clash with canes and coins outside the walls.
At night, undivided, rigid as a tower, with the pride of a lighting flare
  alone amid the blue, the poem, like a sovereign spurning his thrall.

Afterward

In the vain night, earthen, empty and bulbous, the vase
falls with a clatter in the cave. Man falls thus, paralyzed.
In the turbid empire, slave to the fortuity of shadows, he stumbles
    among the rocks from place to place.
Will the present resemble a tomorrow when the lightless season of the
    fall arrives?

As an Epilogue (Com un epíleg, 1980)

Bell

The dead bronze tolls no mass for those who lie still.
The velvet-lined metal in the wilderness's heart
of the time we may yet live speaks only one part.
The other part, timeless, is a snowdrift on a hill.

Midday

Like the bumblebee astray
or the butterfly alight
will our blind eyes see the day?
Will the sun wound us, will night?

Cloud, exploits *in posse*:
delicate, delight slips by.
Lucidity entire, the day
awaits a bird or cry.

As an Epilogue (Com un epíleg, 1980)

Desire

Mad arrows of summer!
Raving, harvesting
the nacre of the lover's body,
the futile smiling silver.

Flickering, there is a river
precise as a diamond.
A desire to be more summer
consumes the lover's body.

Sign

The world is an allegory.
Cabalistic the design
By which the sky absolves
The bird, a substanceless shadow.

Nothing: just a scratch
In the tranquil uniformity
Of the clarified sky.

Clearings! The region
Hides another, concealed
In an invisible script.

As an Epilogue (Com un epíleg, 1980)

Spectacle

The man in white, on the painted cornice, watches as the streets of the seaside city burn. The rituals of fire – crusade, edging, oil – in the eyes of the seafarer: sails, trade winds, a straight pin pressed into the cornea. *Ancor mi raccapriccia.* We will have lived for nothing but a ball of tar in our mouth. For nothing but a burlap rag against our face.

Exile

Pinned to the wall, the sign Nightingale
the sign Goldfinch, names of percussion, of a cry
or Starling, transient of the forests,
a brilliance of images in an instant of words:
light in simulacrum, sound of the word made word. We have uttered
    the yellow afternoon
or the winter hood, the lead basin
of the river filing the ice of the sky,
disaffection of the word and the visible world:
we speak words, but we don't speak the world. Impure, evening cries
    to us
with a weathervane of light in a sky strangled by reds,
venery of signs and falconry of words.
We live not from signs alone, but from signs' sounds;
not from the life of the word, but from the skin of sound.
The veneer of the world in the shadowland of words.

From *The Tempest* (El Vendaval, 1988)

The Gloaming Hour

Rife with mechanisms, tea
and the phonograph on the terrace:
from the avenue, airless,
amber of a liquid that doesn't flee

as darker, neighbors' eyes see
dourly the chase,
and channels of wind embrace
exorcisms, night, and tea.

From *The Tempest* (El Vendaval, 1988)

Plaint

At the hour of desiring no longer to be,
at the hour of desiring most savage,
when the body of the sparrow is ravaged
in a satin abundance of trees;

at the hour of breach and affray –
because love is consigned to disgrace –
violence, this truncheon, lays waste
to the sweetness of yesterday;

at the waiting hour
of the extremity that flowers
in love's spasmodic movements,

scarlet plumage of skin,
prey to linens wherein
the simulacrum, enlarged by love, wounds it,

when, turbid, pleasure burns bright
with the acrid aftertaste of night.

From *The Tempest* (El Vendaval, 1988)

Apotheosis

The gust in the sky scatters timeworn gods,
vine shoots on the turbulent shelf of the sea,
when sulphurous lightning inscribes an X
in the ruby penumbras of signal fires.

Serried light no more defiles the peaks,
or the gem never given, or the crown of the tsar,
or the ribbon of purple on the minaret fixed,
onyx tempest or harrier's eye in the hearth.

The flambant tunics of windblown gods
in a whisper of blood and gold on the rugs,
the prayer of the air for volatile gods:

a gong sounding out in the dolomite nights,
the sword thrust of light of stalactites
and a tumult of Sinbads in Turkesque robes.

Stalking

In small change, like coins tossed
when the riflemen play
the life lent us will be lost,
counted out and repaid.

Passion is a blade that ever
whets us as it hews:
what the nude body fails to sever
is slain by flesh subdued

when we lose our way, and dusk
ingathers our husk
with a black shout of solitude in flames;

to know that we are light, to view
the echoes of a fire anew:
lost Bahamas, forfeited domains.

From *Light* (La llum, 1991)

Testament

Destitute day, conflagration of day,
pink pincers of the violated night,
the towering of daggers in the cat-eyed night
when a poignard reflects the stars' rays,

the feline of night, in the gemstone sky,
this flesh wound of varnish and sulphate,
the rending of a shawl in the gardens of Rabat,
the fingers of radiance a nude body defies:

belly, sun, stars, sex, the rainswept moon.
In our mirror, the gaze of Venus entombed.
With the eyes of the sea the night views us

and light huddles in the beacon of the celestial gloom.
The snow passed below, nineteen hundred's perfume!
A phantasm of dead light on Via Margutta.

Ceremonies

And so we might proceed: from room to room,
perfumed in shadow, as with mint and anise,
with a black rose of ice immured in our teeth,
gloved like the light an amber flask exhumes.

In place of a face, the black rose aforesaid,
and the wing of the snow angel on the tapestry would seethe
where we, like gamepieces in a round of Pachisi,
would live with aromas of gunpowder and lead.

Such regard we would show for the chambers of the air
that the light raining down upon us would dare
to douse with blood a stone of lucid glass;

The whiteness would absorb us as we ask
after the dead, with a shot hushed through damask
or a black dagger in the echoes as I pass.

From *Light* (La llum, 1991)

End

All too true, amassed
in this lilac room, the girls:
while the pink light of Manila curls
in the athenaeum of asps.

All too true, as you lie prone,
divine, and death marauds your eyes
when the lion's eye descries
Chaldean gold disbursed in paper cones.

Vain office, violet and icterine,
vain glimmer, the perse of wine,
here, so true it brings us fright:

All too true, the fairies, yes,
all too real the waves' egress,
and death, so exposed beneath the light

that bowed over the paper's bright demise
in vain I pour out paradise.

Evening

In the salon two claws tear the silk.
Evening steps blind over a game of chess
that a brusque wind scatters, like the flick of a golden cape.
The wax figures, the diorama
of the past, not the image, is the carnage
of memory. I lock,
before a sky stunned by the dry wing beats of eagles,
the bronze deadbolts of night.
And outside, the illusory external empire
shakes torches to conjure the stars.

From *Uncollected Poems* (Poemes esparsos, Darrers poemes, 1995)

Morn

My love, I want nothing but to die in your arms
and life would be a cluster of sweet muscat grapes:
we strain to bear the weight of living;
love swipes with a claw all we've lived through
and shatters it – so much reddened fury,
behind the ivory door of sound, so much pure death
like your arms, like the impure words I speak
when harried by love, splintering life with pick blows,
pleasure and sweetness unfurl my future death.
Death present, death in your arms, like now
at the blue core of the night inspired and clear,
oh my Rosa, oh my Rosa, oh you, rosier still
for you harvest from roses the enduring light
molten and hard, beyond the hour of death
beyond the shadows that laugh haltingly
when bodies lie in the silence of rivers
and we find peace again, and in the death that detains us
we will always be two, statues that one day
will know love, and death binds:
never more, never more separate or distinct, oh supremest
venery of being, neither mascaron nor rag:
you, gospel of light, my life's expiation.

Compact

Lash, lash of time, roaming where the avenues
meet: in a muddled mirror,
not face to face, we will see you waylaid darkly
and then will manage to speak our life – that
thing like silks crushed in the palm.
Never speaking, lone instant of night, your name.

From *Uncollected Poems* (Poemes esparsos, Darrers poemes, 1995)

Lay

Farewell, to you, my delectation...
AUSIAS MARCH

If, from such affliction and so many gems
we learned nothing but to live askance
ever lighting approximate fires,
the sibyl of the waters in the grotto,
mineral words, damp in mute light;
if with so many honed adzes
we learned nothing but to speak words of darkness,
plowing the field, rich with eyes, of the gloom,
the gold with the spectacles of the night,
if we learned but to utter the absent snow
of so many desiccated gales,
if we knew to abstain from the snow
as the rook abstains from the word,
if we are nothing but the thumb of the snow,
aimed at the rock of parched light,
light-parched, snow-parched, and there in the word
we know to speak splendor ablaze in its cages,
like the moribund nightingale telling
when the mares of the darkness will approach.
If from so many censures and conquests
the territory cannot shatter the wasteland,
in the vineyard of the country of air,
like the barrens of the bristling water,
the catafalque of conflagrated clarity,
the church submerged in *Nostalghia*,
the harlequinade of the clarid,
if we do not know the word of the last rites
of dead air, of air buffered by wind,
the plutonic blister of air,
still we know that to live is the Latin
the bird spoke as it chanted to *Percival*,
it is the melodious Latin of leaves,

it is the trilling of luminance
(love: the trilling of luminance),
we know it all, like Chrétien de Troyes
or Carles Riba, we know it all, we clasp
the burning air of obstinacy,
the flickering wick of the bomb
that scorches our hand, the chloratite
of Red Brigades in the Siennese night; Etruscan light
of Etruscan masks in search of the absolute,
the intransigent light of the morning,
the dawn and the night of our love, life:
a red kerchief daubed with blood.

From *The Castle of Purity* (El castell de la puresa, 2014)

The Poet and the Dictator

An extravagant American is in Italy. Better said, a renegade American. His name is Ezra Loomis Pound; readers of poetry know him as Ezra Pound; his friends call him Ezra or Ez even *Old Ez*, not because he is old, but because already, he is a master. And this poet, this reader of outlandish economic tractates, has a hunch that Benito Mussolini may one day turn out useful, for Italy and for the rest of the world. And so he writes him: sends him an eccentric epistle in picturesque and disjointed Italian, his devotion padded out with recondite suggestions, like those of a Renaissance arbitrator addressing a despot or an Italian cardinal. And, so *il Duce* will know who he is dealing with, he includes a selection of poems – typical poems of Pound's, strewn with ciphers, ideograms, fragments in Latin, Greek, Chinese.

The dictator pages through it brutishly: the letter doesn't interest him, its language is strange to him, it's nothing, the frivolities of a rube. But when he reaches the poems, he smiles: *Ma questo è divertente.* This he likes. Getting wind of these words, Pound places the episode in one of his poems: '*Ma questo*, said the Boss, è divertente', and despite all evidence to the contrary, he sees here a sign of the tyrant's portentous lucidity. Such is the fascination of totalitarian power, the temptation of the intellectual to delegate, to displace vicariously, the whole of his moral responsibility onto a leader or system of ideas that seems to subsume the external world beneath an all-embracing organisational system. This delegation, which relieves the burden of judgment, is never disadvantageous to power. Years later, Soviet grandstanders wished to ban the work of a deceased poet: Mayakovsky. The woman the poet loved, Lilya Brik, besought Stalin to protect it. As though dropping a coin into an automat, she achieved her purpose by spluttering a formula: 'Mayakovsky is the greatest poet of the Soviet era.' The protection extended took the standard form of an official cliché, salvaging Mayakovsky by transforming him into a puppet useful for the validation of despotism. In essence, the words 'the greatest', or the simple verdict 'divertente', display the same contempt, the same distrust, reserved by the politician for the poet.

14 October 1979

I am Still Learning

Francisco de Goya arrived in Bordeaux in 1824. Deaf, debilitated, unable to speak a word of French, without a valet or servant of any sort. Goya's friends feared the French winter, harsher than that of Madrid, would kill him. Weak and ungainly, he endangered himself when he went out to walk the streets, and yet the very thing that interested him was *not* to travel by coach, to see the strange and picturesque things that formed, in part, the vision of the world, at once ironic, burlesque, bitter, and cordial, that he had arrived at over the years. In company, Goya was a braggart: he said he might live to ninety-nine, like Titian, and two months before his eightieth birthday, he recollected the bullfights he'd taken part in during his youth, declaring that even now, with a sword in his hand, he would cower in fear before no one. He painted and drew incessantly, and corrected none of what he'd done. But that arrogant old man knew the truth: in a letter to a friend, he confessed he was blind, his pulse was weak, and there was nothing left to him but an excess of will.

It is this hoary Goya, the giant on the verge of collapse, but still powerful, and grander than ever in the final splendors of his passion for doing and being, who draws on black stone with a crayon, most likely with an eye to publishing the results – the technique, lithography, had only just then been invented – a pair of moving albums. The most stunning image they contain is the figure of a robust, bearded man over a black background, reminiscent of Father Time, walking forward, his expression stubborn, determined, with the aid of two canes. The artist's hand, still sure, has left to preside over the composition a title at once explanation and anthem: *Aún aprendo*, I am still learning. Yes, Goya is still learning, and not only the technique of lithography. Walled up in in his deafness, he is learning to live at a time when reasonably he should start learning to die.

Learning, if we believe in it, lasts as long as life itself, and breaks off brusquely, should we ever cease to believe.

19 October 1979

From the *Dietari 1979–1982*

A Sorcerer's Disappearance

One uncertain day, sometime in the mid-twenties, a young Ernest Hemingway is sitting on the terrace of the café La Closerie des Lilas in Paris. A shriveled man in a cape walks past in the company of a tall girl, glances furtively at the guests, doesn't stop to stare, vanishes. A friend of Hemingway's, present at the time, tells the author: 'That's Aleister Crowley, the diabolist. He's supposed to be the wickedest man in the world.'

Several years later, the same man, with the same cape and the same girl – a German by the name of Hanni L. Jaeger – reaches port in Lisbon. The month is September, the year 1930. Imposing, the man in the cape – with 'malicious, satanic eyes', we are told – greets an acquaintance who is standing there waiting for him: a timid character, faint of heart, an aficionado of the occult, whom he only knows from correspondence. There was fog, and the ship has reached Lisbon twenty-four hours late. Crowley, sardonic, playing his role to the hilt, greets his Portuguese friend with the words: 'What possessed you to send this fog my way?'

It is an ambiguous reproach, part wry, part conciliatory, bearing an allusion to their shared interest in necromancy. This tone will define the two men's relationship. The Englishman is a complex figure: spy and agent provocateur for the English government during the First World War; magician, astrologer, theosopher, millenarian, a freemason even, apparently. He has traveled in India and China; in Bombay, it is said, he killed a native to drink his blood, but this may be an unfounded rumor; he is known by the titles Master Therion and The Beast 666, the same one identified in the Book of Revelations. He speaks Greek and Latin. The Portuguese, dark and secretive, is named Fernando Pessoa; many years after his death, the world will know him as a great poet.

The episode ended rather absurdly, with the sorcerer vanishing in seemingly enigmatic circumstances, leaving behind a message in theosophical code. Pessoa drew on the occasion for a series of extraordinary hypotheses that attracted the attention of members of the press. Naturally, it was all smoke and mirrors (the matter is too convoluted to summarise here), and a year later, Pessoa will write to a friend: 'Crowley, who went to live in Germany after his suicide, wrote me the other day...' Still, the supposed disappearance of the sorcerer, and the alternate panic and humor he provoked in Pessoa, are representative of one of every poet's hidden desires: the thing Nerval called 'the expansion of dreams into life'. To achieve it by appealing to the complicity of a sorcerer of a more or less farcical character – or, to be precise, farcical on occasions, but not always, and not in all things, evidently – is a path less sincere than poetic invention and less hazardous than alcohol or hallucinogens. And yet it has a double advantage: it is a path that impends effectively on exterior reality, and at the same time, allows for a margin of ambiguity (and a means of return, if necessary) concerning that which is and that which is not. As Pessoa himself says in a short poem of his:

The poet is a faker
His fakery so complete
He suffers as the maker
From the pain of his conceit.

21 October 1979

A Russian in Paris

If you find yourself in the Place de la Concorde, you may walk toward the Seine and the sumptuous, ghostly Pont Alexandre with its petrified luxury of verdigris and gold, or else, with your back to the river, step out onto onto the Rue Royale, passing by the door of Maxim's, which is now, in essence, an international restaurant, but the utterance of the mere name of which continues to evoke figures from Colette, strutting personages drunk on champagne, glimmering with precious stones. Or you can turn right, and will pass beneath the arches of the Hôtel de la Marine – a distant memory of cannons and bombards, the pure silence of veils in the Martinican sky – which will soon bring you out onto Rue de Rivoli.

The arcades stretch on and on. At the far end glimmers the gate – iron spears, black and gold – of the Tuileries gardens. Here, along the covered passageway, the Rue de Rivoli is almost exclusively commercial, its shops not so costly as those of the Fauborg Saint-Honoré, closer to Maxim's, but still glamorous and varied enough in kind to arouse the curiosity or greed of the foreigners lodging in the Ritz or the Intercontinental who, without walking far, will inevitably end up standing before this solemn, alluring, unbroken row of display windows. Everything is impeccably cared for beneath the ancient and noble stone of the archways, everything seems sparkling new. All at once, a plaque appears on the wall – gilded letters on a backdrop of black stone, if memory serves – telling you that this street, too, has a story. The plaque commemorates the house where Count Leo Tolstoy lived for a season in Paris.

Often, Tolstoy's characters – like Dosteovsky's, among others – converse in French, following the custom among the cultivated of their century, particularly in Russia and Poland. This is true even for discussions of trivial matters. It is natural then that certain of Tolstoy's protagonists – like Pierre in *War and Peace* – are only fully graspable as people who inhabited the France of the Encyclopedists, the Revolution, and Romanticism, but who did so from the heart of the Slavic world; people who – in a literal sense, but also, clearly, in a figurative one – think in French. Our tendency however is to imagine Tolstoy as somehow remoter, kin to the nights of Petersburg or Moscow, the mute repose of the snowy plains, the distant, barbarous luxury of horses amid the cold, cutting clarity of the grasslands.

Such a landscape was the setting of the writer's mature years and his moving, solitary death. The Tolstoy who, in 1857, lived in an elegant house alongside the Tuileries on Rue de Rivoli – everything a Russian nobleman in Paris could ask for – was a twenty-nine-year-old man who had yet to publish his greatest novels, and who came to recognise, during that stay in Paris, all the things that bound him to and separated him from Western Europe. Fifty-three years later, senile, in his eighties, Tolstoy, who decides one day to run away from home during the harsh Russian autumn, is a man who will brook no compromise between his morals and day-to-day life.

He runs away, and leaves a letter telling his wife he has done so in order 'to go on living alone with my conscience'. At five in the morning on 28 October 1910, in the company of his doctor and daughter, Alexandra, the old man leaves his house undercover and spends the night in a monastery. He will still have time to write a long article on the death penalty; but his implacable family is close on his heels, and he must hurry through the stages of his journey. On the train, he falls ill, and has to stop at a station in the provinces, where he will die on November 20. At first, this solitary, persecuted man, agonising in an obscure Russian train station, seems the furthest thing from that young aristocrat passing a season in a Parisian mansion. But if we look at the august letters on the plaque in the Rue de Rivoli – the only tangible reminder of the Russian count's presence in Paris – we may perhaps be allowed to muse that, in a certain way, the agonising Russian patriarch and the dazzling nobleman, hungry to see and know France, are complementary rather than opposite. The one explains the other, because they have in common the desire to live truthfully.

21 November 1979

From the *Dietari 1979–1982*

The Enemy Within

'Time is the evil', we read in a poem by Ezra Pound. And it is, certainly. But, powerful as it may be, it is only external. There is another adversary, still more terrible, more devastating: the enemy within. It will not ravage us physically, like time, but may annihilate us inside. Ausiàs March saw as much at the close of the fifteenth century, and he described the experience in this way:

> *Badly lives he*
> *who has thought as his enemy...*

For what arms do we dispose of to combat our own thoughts? If thought turns against us, it finds an armory inside us: it assails us with insomnia, depression, neurosis, excitability, with that mania for labor that prevents the mind from finding repose, or with lassitude, so we live mechanically, like sleepwalkers. But its greatest danger is the covertness of its hostility. When conflict turns pathological, we may draw the enemy into pitched battle. But should we do so, should we insist on doing so, when our adversary seems to be nothing more than thought, which, however pernicious and destructive, remains within the limits of what we take to be normal? This is a literal example of a 'wicked thought', not the kind we are warned about in Sunday school, but another, far deeper, far graver sort. It is the enemy within, that part of ourselves that brings us to grief, that makes us lose sight of what we are. Persistent, tenacious, thoughts revisit us impertinently; we cannot hold them at bay; silently, they govern our comings and goings, cast their shadow over our judgments, walk eternally at our side. Our enemies, they subvert us in silence. We may wrestle against them, like Jacob against the angel; there is no saying whether the struggle will ever end.

One of the highest purposes of literature is a kind of moral hygiene with respect to thoughts. Putting them in writing, we establish their precise limits, demarcate the outer edges of their domain, map them, expose them. At times, we may fail to put them into words, but we can almost always suggest their presence obliquely, and in any case, writing forces us to set out clearly – even to ourselves – our relationship to the thoughts that govern our conduct. Not the mirror carried along a road that the novel represented for Stendhal, but a mirror in which our conscience sees itself. The extreme tension of moral poetry – in Ausiàs March, in Baudelaire, in Carles Riba, in J.V. Foix – proceeds from the effort to apprehend a clear image in this mirror.

2 December 1979

A Toast

This time – on 15 February 1893 – it was a poet presiding over the banquet. A toast was *de rigueur,* and naturally, it was expected that the poet would offer one in verse. And so he rose from his seat; on his lips was a soft, subtle half-smile; his gaze was vague, as though intent on a distant daydream. Everyone thought him nervous, ill at ease before so many eyes. Resolute, he took his glass and began to recite a poem. His voice was sonorous, textured, but wavering: not the voice of a man accustomed to think of verse as something to be uttered in public and aloud. The poem was brief, and was received with three ovations in succession. Slightly surprised, the poet heard the echoes of the applause. Outside, the Paris sky was frozen and clear.

What can a poet say in a toast? After all, the time of the elegant poetry of the baroque is past, the time when – at the court of a lesser Italian noble, or in some surly and solitary palace – any theme served as a canvas for the execution of a bit of verbal filigree: a portrait of the concept in the mind, of sound arranged in rhythm. Nor are we in a medieval tavern, with vagabond goliards chanting in corrupted Latin, or one of those palaces where the troubadours crooned their winged versicles, gentle and sweet. No: we are in the final act of the nineteenth century, in a big, enigmatic, faceless city, where tenderness abides only in select recondite refuges. And the poet, at the moment of toasting, is simply a man, a glass of champagne clutched in his hand. And he must talk about his glass, this glass which will make of him a person absurd or majestic: on what he can manage to say of a thing as fragile and fleeting as a glass of champagne will depend, at that moment, the triumph or the triviality of poetry.

Triviality? Poetry may not be much more profound – or more trivial – than this thing: champagne in a glass. Inside or perhaps overflowing the crystal, white foam capping the luster of liquefied gold. Nothing, foam… That is:

Rien, cette écume.

Yes, the toast must begin thus: with the foam – which is nothing – in the glass. Saying, then, from the beginning, that it is nothing.

Everything that comes afterward will be the exclusive proceeds of the poem.

Five years later, a few weeks before his death, the poet – Stéphane Mallarmé, retired English teacher – gave his final indications concerning the ordering of his poems. Pride of place – the portico, the prelude, if you prefer: the point of access, the entrance, but also, in a way, a declaration of what is to be his work's overarching tone – is granted to that toast, distinguished by its airiness, to a piece that appeared merely circumstantial. *It is nothing, this foam...* The nothing, the foam – the invisible, the transitory, inexistent were it not for an existence imparted by the power of the word – stands at the beginning of the work, just as, toward the end, in the last poem Mallarmé would write, the significance of emptiness will equal that of the printed letters. From nothing to nothing: in a pause, in a blank space, foam. Nothing: a poem. Our word.

27 December 1979

Simulacra

The Latin poet Lucretius dedicates practically an entire book of his poem to the discussion of simulacra. A simulacrum is like an appearance; for Lucretius, an Epicurean, 'all things have what we call simulacra: a kind of slight membrane that comes away from the surfaces of their bodies and whirls here and there through the air'. With these words, which I am pleased to translate according to my whims, begins, in Book IV of *De Rerum Natura*, the explanation of what simulacra are. An explanation which, in some ways, has never been surpassed. This fantastical and essentially magical physics of slight membranes may make us laugh, even if, more or less, until the eighteenth century, science gave credence to things with not much more basis in fact; still, the discourse we find in Lucretius on the effects of simulacra on human behavior gives us highly exact information about the influence of fantastical mirages on the passions. Proceeding intuitively, feeling his way along, Lucretius discerns, no less clearly than the moralists and psychoanalysts, the action of the springs of our conduct. Everything – in Lucretius or in psychoanalysis – may be summed up in terms of desire, in the broadest sense of the word: if we desire simulacra, it is because they are external, and the impulse toward simulacra is of a piece with that impulse which, in puberty, drives us toward fusion with all that appears different from ourselves and for that reason calls to us and attracts us.

There is a poetic truth deeper than scientific or material truth, and it is to this that Lucretius aspires. What he says about simulacra moves us, even when we know it to be based on hypotheses science has declared false; it moves us by its admirable acuity of observation and the delicacy of its expression. What simulacrum is clearer than the erotic dreams of adolescence? 'Adolescents, pervaded with the fecund fluid of youth, once the generating seed has ripened in their bodies, are drawn toward those simulacra a beautiful face and seductive colours offer to them,' we read. Yes – and Lucretius's way of saying this is crude and tender equal parts, and that is no easy thing – these simulacra push us to possess them, because 'passion turns toward the object that has inflicted the wound of love. Because the law dictates that the wounded man shall lie down by the wounded woman: blood flows in the direction of the person who has wounded...' And so 'this is Venus for us, this is the reality we call love; this is the spring that spatters sweetly and drop by drop works its way into our hearts and will later freeze us with sorrow. Because, if the beloved is absent, we always keep an image of it near us...'

Yet, Lucretius rushes to add, simulacra of this kind are to be avoided, we must slake our amorous thirst with whomever we come across, rather than concentrating on an individual who may well make us suffer. In this way, he pays tribute to his inner Epicurean: but what comes first – the description, in dreams or waking, of the mirages of love and desire, of the languor, the fury, the longing they inspire – is likely something else: the tribute the poet Lucretius pays to the passions of Lucretius the man. The philosopher tells himself, and tells us, not to let the simulacra carry us away; the poet, the man, knows and feels obscurely, just as we all do, that at times some simulacra are stronger than any philosophy, and that the entirety of our lives may perhaps be conceived as a measureless simulacrum: wounding, intermittently sweet.

19 January 1980

From the *Dietari 1979–1982*

Facts and Morals

Some people are fascinated by facts; others by the world of ideas, of thought – not by facts themselves, but by their moral significance. There are writers, even admirable ones, who limit themselves to matters of fact. Of the thousands upon thousands of pages of Saint-Simon's memoirs, it may be said that they contain only the details of external events; there is thought, but only of a kind required to emphasise the materiality, the graphical force, the visual weight of facts. Saint-Simon does nothing more than describe, with the greatest possible intensity and precision, what he has seen or what others have told him. Things seen and things heard, that is all; like those spies who were the eyes and ears of bygone sovereigns, Saint-Simon becomes the reader's eyes and ears. We see, we feel, the cold of stone and brilliancy of the torches in the corridors of Versailles, the game meat served after dinner, almost at midnight, with harp and lute music and the flicker of candles in the grand candelabra; in a courtyard, bare and soft beneath the sky, a horse's whinny, the transient flash of spurs; far off, the thread of the horizon, the dust cloud of the troops retiring to their winter quarters. There are characters, too: grotesque or vain, brutishly lascivious, or truculent and embittered: marshals, dukes, surgeons, bishops, actors. To read Saint-Simon is to live all of that.

Other writers, more severe, are only interested in the sharp outlines of moral life. This may even be true of narrators devoted to the facts, provided their subject is not an indifferent one. Stendhal's sensuality, his feeling for beauty, his capacity for suggesting, in a genuine and deeply discriminating way, the most fragile of sentiments and – moreover – the precise and implacable facts, should not blind us to a certain purposive opacity in the surface of his novels. Everything in *The Red and the Black*, and particularly in *The Charterhouse of Parma*, would constitute a crowded, motley, captivating spectacle, had Stendhal observed it with the eyes of Saint-Simon; and, as a good reader of Saint-Simon, he undoubtedly possessed the necessary instincts, the requisite aptitudes, for compositions of this sort. But more pressing for him was the need to evaluate all that he noted down in moral terms. He was was not of the race of chroniclers and memorialists, but of the race of men of ideas.

Open, at random, any volume of Saint-Simon, to whatever page you see fit; you will undoubtedly have there everything you need; the fragment you read will be self-sustaining, will not refer in any essential way to anything beyond itself; isolated, it will possess an adequate power of seduction, because every line of Saint-Simon is a vehicle transmitting, with unusual vigor, his extraordinary receptive and retentive genius vis-à-vis external events. Now try the same experiment with Stendhal: true, you will admire the precision of style, but you will not manage to escape the impression that this fragment, taken on its own, is inert, or almost insert, because the author's attention clings not to the immediate plastic qualities of the scene described, but to a moral examination of the aggregate, of the broadest portion of experience of which these things are components.

Sanseverina, or Julien Sorel, or Fabrizio del Dongo, or Count Mosca, are unforgettable thanks to an accumulation of details, a residue they leave behind – the famed *détails exacts* – thanks to a sediment of acquaintance built up in the course of the book, an almost unconscious progression of a kind that characterises many people we come across in life; whereas any character from Saint-Simon – be he omnipresent and formidable as Louis XIV or some flunky viewed askance in a courtesan's bedchamber – leaps to the eye as if drawn on the page, like a spring-loaded jester popping out of its box. This is Saint-Simon's subject: the present, the irreducible present, lived and preserved in memory. It demands nothing more, and in this lies its vigor. Stendhal, on the other hand, through small, subtle touches, wishes to show the gears, the threads that connect one event to the other, and generate, in the process, an ethical mechanism. If you prefer it put simply, Saint-Simon is the extravert, Stendhal the introvert.

The synthesis will come later: in Proust, the intensity of perception of isolated things is as powerful as in Saint-Simon; at the same time, the moral tension is as acute, as closely observed, as in Stendhal.

2 January 1980

From the *Dietari 1979–1982*

The American Poet

An American poet? No, something more: *the* American poet. Not in an ethnic, national, racial sense. Let us be more sensible, more modest. American literature – the literature of the United States – has a group of poets who have entered the awareness of our countrymen late, in fragments, and haphazardly. To attempt to define *the* American poet is not a trivial game, at least, not only and not completely. Let us revise a bit the question at hand: the American poet – or any country's poet – is not an absolute, but rather a preference of each one of us. The history of taste is the history of preferences. To say *our* American poet – to say *my* American poet – is to proffer a signal, a symptom.

Some will think of remoter poets, those from the nineteenth century: delicate and tender Longfellow, or sonorous and glacial Poe, who has the curious virtue of appealing almost exclusively to foreigners. Others, more exalted, will think of Walt Whitman: reckless, vast, encyclopedic, at the same time deeply gentle beneath his severity, like an old tree under rough bark, or the echo of a chorus of waves overheard in a dark, barren cave. Some will look to Emily Dickinson, who lived as if drenched in water and exposed to the icy air of death or the expansive fire of infinitude – in the bliss of verdant grass and petals weighed down with dew. Old images, as if engraved on boxwood.

Our century has other poets. Ezra Pound, *il miglior fabbro*, disordered genius, coarse like a badly polished gem, a prodigy of gesticulation and disarray, rough draft of a prospective Homer gone too early to seed, a puzzle of ill-fitting pieces; perhaps this is why he fascinates us, because he allows to imagine the possible poems sketched out in his magnetic flow of words. There are the *patrician Americans*, as Gabriel Ferrater used to call them: wise, agrarian Robert Frost, strict and noble Robert Lowell. And William Carlos Williams, playful and precise. Then there is the banker, eternally endued with a certain workaday air, a functionary of poetry, Anglicising and Anglicised – we imagine him in a bowler, holding a black leather briefcase – and yet, when he wants, he is deliriously dramatic, intimate with the atavism of fear immemorial, of dusty, dreadful myth: T.S. Eliot.

American poets, certainly. But the most guarded among them – and, why not say it, *my* American poet – is not quite so well known as they. He was a shadowy, discreet man, an assiduous subscriber to French magazines who never traveled to Europe and barely budged from the town where he lived. He was vice president of an insurance company and his name was Wallace Stevens. This fall will be the centenary of his birth; next summer, it will be twenty-five years since his death. He did not care for much to be known of his life; in his words, he had done nothing but study law and live in Hartford, and these facts struck him as neither compelling nor relevant.

The Catalan world lacks, to my knowledge, even a minimally satisfactory edition of Wallace Stevens in translation. A dozen or more years back, a brief bilingual anthology was published in Spanish in Argentina. Now, in Barcelona, Plaza & Janés has published another one, likewise bilingual, and far more extensive, selected by a poet from the Canary Islands, Andrés Sánchez Robayna – whose ties to Catalonia, incidentally, are very deep. The excerpts are representative of Stevens, who is an absolutely exquisite poet, elliptical, characterised by outlines subtly arranged against a completely stark background. There is nothing of sinuosity: the poet's words aim straight for the essential, the nucleus, so vivid and variable that often, like an optical illusion, we do not see it at first glance. This nucleus is – as with the greatest poets – a purely mental and strictly sensuous time: luminous visions, exotic, shadowed, abstract, unbound from everything that is not pure existence as image and the hint of sound, or else a flickering swordplay of ideas and concepts growing clearer in the *camera obscura* of the mind as it invents the poem. Inevitably, it all flows together: the poem is the spectacle – mental and sensuous – of the process of poetry's creation, analogous to the development of a photographic negative, in which the contrast, vaguely silver, wavers between black and white, mutating progressively into the splendor of clearly defined colours, concise and tender or powerful and imposing, as the case may be. The brilliance of this consummate intelligence, of this incomparably refined sensibility, is a tension in the pure and dazzling air.

12 February 1980

The Pistol and the Drawing Rooms

No: you will no longer find this poet in the country. As a young man, he lived in the country, and in a letter he spoke of gulleys, of the high, noble, solitary flight of eagles, of the extensive, undulating verdure of the steppes. In those days, he writes, he used to nourish himself on mute sentiments and on the beauty of the countryside. He knew the cloud-crested summits, the snowdrifts, the green of the gardens, the deepest blue of the sea beneath the brightest blue of the sky. But now you will find him in drawing rooms. In a poem, he offers a description of them: aristocrats, soldiers, gallants, ladies in sumptuous dress, complacent beneath the light of crystal chandeliers. Look, it's like a painting: the lady of the house surrounded – as if in a makeshift frame – by a group of impeccable gentlemen, talking with the scrupulous vacancy of automata. Aloof, one man contemplates the room as though looking down on a group of ghosts. This man – is he the poet? If he is, it is only inwardly, only in the marrow – tense and corrosive, or glacially empty – of his conscience. Because, on the surface, he seems to fit in perfectly, to be fashioned of the same stuff – the drunkenness of chandelier light, the drunkenness of gaming tables, the drunkenness of nacre in the fans – as that friction of murmurs and dazzling garments in the Saint Petersburg night. A friend of his tells us: 'I only ever meet Pushkin at balls. And he will continue in this way, wasting his life, unless something compels him to go elsewhere.'

Elsewhere. Six years before, Pushkin had finished a narrative poem, *Eugen Onegin*. I would like linger now over an episode from this poem. It is day, and the sun is shining over the snowy landscape. Onegin hurries out of bed, helped by a French manservant. This morning, Onegin has an appointment, which he arrives to in a sleigh. He carries a box with a pistol inside, a Lepage, the best-known brand among the elegant set in the Russia of the time. Now they are arrived: beside a mill, beneath the oaks, on a clear, cold day. Onegin has come for a duel with a young poet. Onegin – is he Pushkin? And the young poet – is he not, in a certain way, Pushkin, too? The pistols glimmer; the bullets are snug now against the rifling in the barrel. Onegin fires, and the poet falls. Onegin feels a strange chill; he has wounded the poet mortally.

The poet's mind is dark and hushed, like an abandoned house with closed shutters: one of those houses in Russia where they streak the windows with lime to block the sun during the long months of solitude.

Now look: we are in the outskirts of Saint Petersburg during the last days of January 1837. This time it is Pushkin who has an appointment, with his brother-in-law, a French émigré: D'Anthès, an officer of the Imperial Guard. The time for composing verses while listening to Rossini has passed; now is the hour to look a fate we presage hazily in the face, as if through darkness, as if woven into the fabric of a poem. Pushkin walks forward, his pistol pointed at the ground. D'Anthès – unmoving, fixed as an obsession – fires. A hole, black and bloody, appears in Pushkin's chest, and he falls now, on this frosty morning in the outskirts of Saint Petersburg, just as the young poet fell beneath the oaks, not far from the millwheel, amid the frigid solitude of the fields.

The Almanach de Gotha of 1838 is a tiny volume containing a yearly inventory of wins and losses among the worldly; it records the landslides and the minimal seismic shifts in the static, rigid era of the frivolous aristocracy and the gallantry of the drawing rooms. There is a curt line buried deep in the Almanach de Gotha that recollects the day in 1837 when the Russian poet Alexander Pushkin, of noble origins, died as the consequence of a duel. The letters are minuscule, but the words have a dry and abrupt report, like a pistol fired in the brilliance of a drawing room on the night of a ball.

8 March 1980

From the *Dietari 1979–1982*

The Mulatta and the Dandy

Beneath the portrait of the mulatta, the dandy has written the Latin words: *Quaerens quem devoret*. Is this a dictum, an insignia? Long ago, horsemen used to enter the tourney with their faces covered, identifiable only by the colours of their garments and shield and the curt, laconic enchantment of a motto. We read, for example, in *Curial and Guelfa: Lover without beloved – Desire before piety – A wayward heart knows no home*, and we imagine those knights, darkly clothed with black shields, entering the fray under a bright day's sky, with a flash of metal, of horseshoes and lances that wounds the eyes of the ladies seated on the risers.

But now, there is nothing in the world that can wound these eyes: they are eyes with the 'heavy brilliance of somber ponds and the unguent calm of tropical seas'. The woman is 'black and luminous', bright like a beacon, with the yellowish, pallid glimmer of gas lamps in the febrile, ailing Parisian night. Yes: the mulatta, ambling in the world of evening, is a tigress, a vampire, or an Amazon, or even more, the blue aloofness of the lunar glow, which has, in the dark corners of the immense, putrescent city, a very soft scuffing of silk about it, slight and ravenous: *Quaerens quem devoret*. The words are old, from the First Epistle of Saint Peter: 'Your adversary the devil, as a roaring lion, walketh about, seeking whom he may devour'. Here, in the 'the hidden stairway of the bedchamber', the relationship between Jeanne Duval and Charles-Pierre Baudelaire is like the relationship of the lion to his prey. The sullen beauty devours the dandy in the stifling velvets of the dressing room, where the rarefied air sticks in the throat, amid perfumed, acrid shadows, muffling all thought of a hoarse cry.

We know what Baudelaire looked like: a man with pink gloves, long, dyed hair tucked in a ringlet behind his ear, ankle boots so shiny he could use them as a mirror – and he does so, he likes to look at himself in them, at his frail, fearless figure: a spectral apparition, a frozen figment, like a face in a cameo. He has been spotted walking up the embankment of the Namur Gate: on tiptoe, zigzagging to avoid stepping in the filth, or hopping in the rain, intangible in his white shirt, or dressed, like an actor, in a baggy houppelande. He lived in permanent familiarity with elegance, at a place and time where doing so became both an ascetic discipline and a controlled and almost stoic sort of obscenity. More than perverse, the dandy is a moralist: he makes of elegance a school, a life project, rigorous, based in a certain way on the transmutation of lived matter, on a meticulous and systematic exaltation that might seem gratuitous, did it not sustain a form of ethical passion. A form of religion, in a manner of speaking, devoid of religious faith, but potent and functional nonetheless. 'Even if it were proven', the dandy writes, 'that God didn't exist, religion would still be saintly and divine.' Is this a provocation? No more so than his association of the mulatta Jeanne Duval – his obsession, the guiding specter or erotic fetish at his life's center – with the lion from the distant sacred epistle. There is a deep moral truth at the heart of the dandy's construct of elegance and eccentricity: the intuition, lucidly expressed, of an analogy between inner experience and eroticism conceived as part of a life framed deliberately, unswervingly in terms of moral evaluation.

We know where the dandy was born: on the corner of Rue Hautefeuille and Boulevard Saint-Germain. The house was demolished in one of those feverish fits of urban renewal Paris is prone to. Now, the Rue Hautefill boasts four small cinemas, all in the same complex. Toward evening, when the sky is still bright – of a soft blue, textured and luminous, or else of a wet pearl grey – next to a bookstore devoted to the esoteric and occult, there are four lines of people, not very long, awaiting the start of the show. Each line leads to a different cinema, but the boundaries between them are blurred, uncertain at times: you have to trace out a modest itinerary, sketch out precisely, on a map in the mind, the topography of the place. At the end of a hallway, or at the top of the stairs, you are surprised by the sudden appearance of the screen, unexpected, exultantly bright in the darkness. No: even now, Baudelaire is not so far away, because what we see here is 'the clear fire that fills the lucid spaces'. And are these pallid silvery shadows on the virgin celluloid not, perhaps, 'living pillars, uttering at times words confused'? Do we not see here a 'forest of symbols'?

When we step out on the street, it is already rather cold: maybe it has rained a bit, a fine rain like a shiver coating the streets and the terraces of the cafes. A river of faces passes on the boulevard. When Baudelaire had already been dead for three years, Nadar, the photographer – the man who, on an afternoon at the theater, had introduced the young Baudelaire to the mulatta actress a quarter-century before – sees a singular figure on the boulevards: Jeanne Duval, old, walking on crutches and talking alone. No one saw her again. We may suppose that Nadar, the photographer, turned his head and followed her with his eyes. Laid low, but never vanquished, the dark goddess prowled like the lion Baudelaire had glimpsed. Look: already she is far away. The maws of Paris have devoured yet another shadow.

9 March 1980

The Bedroom of the Poetess

We can see this bedroom now. Of course, it is no longer inhabited; it has become a museum, a place of pilgrimage. It is bare, with a crucifix hung over the headboard of a nineteenth-century bed, of old wood, noble and severe. At its foot, on the floor, is a large vase of flowers. But what most catches the eye is the window in this photo I am now examining. The curtains, solemn and translucent – suspended in the immobile clarity of air – open onto a vivid splendor which we can only intuit – something compact, vague, and powerful. It is the brightness of day in the landscape outside, just as the poetess saw it, with eyes already frail, in this bedroom where she died, with a savor of light in the silence of the courtyard, prolonged in the verdant stillness of the olive trees.

Rosalía de Castro was already dying on 15 July 1885, when she asked to be brought a bouquet of pansies, the flowers she loved most. She held them close to her lips, and felt breathless; eyes clouded, she told her eldest daughter, 'Open the window. I want to see the sea'. Yes, the same window we are looking at now, this window whose curtains hint at the insurrection of light; but this window doesn't open onto the sea. Did she see it, perhaps, with other eyes, with inward eyes, purer and more serene? Perhaps, in her interior, this gaze of mind and spirit, at the moment of transit toward death – for these were her final words – she opened herself to life with another intensity, with a different sort of duration. The dimension of memory, perhaps, and even of a particular memory, still precise and vital – because we know when Rosalía had last seen the sea. It was on a journey of leavetaking, a goodbye to the salt and foam and waves; and on the last day, as they were soon to leave the port, her husband – how much we know of this husband, and at the same time, how little! – recalls Rosalía standing up in her compartment, the window cracked, waiting from second to second for the train to set in motion. The sun, the same sun that shines on the beach we have just left, the life-giving sun on the bright and saline murmurs of the shore, lights up her face: a face weary, not beautiful, but with a firm and tranquil inner tension that recaptured a shadow of fleeting peace amid that seaside brilliance.

The train has left; Rosalía will venture, shadow among shadows, into the garden, the courtyard, where, sullen and serene, the olive trees

From the *Dietari 1979–1982*

fall silent. Did Rosalía see the sea? The room is empty now, but in the curtains, in the day, the light carries reverberations from the water on a faraway shore. If you close your eyes, do you not hear, very soft, in the lustrous air, in the rustle of the leaves, the lapping of waves in this abandoned bedroom?

11 March 1980

Beginnings

Herman Melville opens *Moby Dick* with an abrupt, direct appeal to his readers: 'Call me Ishmael.' A splendid beginning, justifiably famous. We already know what the book will be: a narration of events experienced by a man like us, who speaks to us; a man with a story, who takes a borrowed name, as if to say one name is no better or worse than any other. Or perhaps – if we consider him more closely – a man inclined to take a moniker freighted with biblical resonances, because in the story he has to tell us, the core of moral symbolism matters more than the outer crust of events; he asks us to call him Ishmael because with this name, we come closer to the vital nucleus of the tale.

Could you ask for an opening greyer, more conventional, more neutral – at first glance – than Stendhal's in *The Red and the Black?* Stendhal writes: 'The little town of Verrières may be considered among the comeliest in all Franche-Comté.' Is this not the banality of a tour guide? It is plain to see that Monsieur Beyle, who signed his name Stendhal, used to read a half-hour of the good dry prose of the Napoleonic Code before settling down to write from one day to the next. The beginning of *The Red and the Black,* which seems so anodyne, is a rigorous artifice of genius: it announces an implacable, impeccable neutrality, a refined and deliberate – but inwardly taut – capacity for exposition that will reveal, as in the quote from Danton we read in the novel's frontispiece, 'the truth, the bitter truth'.

And Proust? In a novel built of long phrases, ample periods – volutes, arabesques, calligraphy of mind and senses – the first brief sentence has something almost Stendhalian in its precision: 'When I was young, I used to go to bed early.' Another masterly example of apparent triviality, because what Proust does with this first phrase – which, as we know, he didn't settle on before sketching out and revising many drafts – is immobilise the attention, fix it in a zone of experience – the bedtime hour, the moment of struggle against insomnia and the specters of memory – that presents, in miniature, the entire process he will lay out through the three thousand long pages of his work: that of a man faced with a moral spectacle set before him by memory.

Beyond simple neutrality, we have the beginning of Kafka's *The Castle:*

'It was late evening when K. arrived.' The maximum of information in the least number of words: an individual, known only by the initial K., has made a journey, has left, has arrived at some place not clear to us; when he gets there, it is already almost dark; all this, moreover, happens in a not very concrete past, which may be the conventional past of the majority of novels, but may also – bare and abstract as it is – points toward something else. Where did K. come from? Where did he arrive to? When did all of this occur? Might it be now, when we are reading? We will finish *The Castle* without answers to these questions this first line provokes. Perhaps the response is inside us. K. doesn't reach the castle, and the novel remains unfinished, because the world is circular, and the past tense of K.'s arrival is the present tense of our arrival at the book. K. is us.

25 March 1980

Le Carré and Simenon

Both fascinate us, and not because they are, in genre terms, 'crime novelists'. Crime fiction may be good literature: think of Dashiell Hammett or Raymond Chandler. Still, Hammett and Chandler are good literature of an indubitably local type. Of the United States, naturally, of life in small towns or of the intrigues of the capital cities. Simenon and Le Carré, on the other hand, are good European literature. They feel closer to us.

Both have something willfully grey about them. The characters they manipulate are opaque: Commissioner Maigret and Le Carré's George Smiley are both intelligent, but of a vulgar, stodgy nature. They never intervene in exotic affairs; we see them amid the sorrow and tedium of everyday things, as people who abhor these things with the curious resignation of those who have no choice but to dwell among them. And their settings, far away as they may be, form part of a more restricted horizon than may be apparent at first.

The world of Simenon's characters is the former French Empire. That of Le Carré's is the residue or ghost of the former British one. With time, the thread of the French colonies gets lost, and thenceforward, the scope of Simenon's novels shrinks progressively: they speak only of a mansion, a town, a small city, some neighborhood. Perhaps even simply of a family, a street, a pension – in this way, they are vast and microscopic as the novels of Balzac.

The British Empire disintegrates as well. But Le Carré's world narrows and expands at the same time. It expands: things happen in Hamburg and Moscow and London and Paris simultaneously, or else in Hong Kong and Moscow and London and Peking. Everything is directed, registered, observed, controlled from different places. Everything has echoes elsewhere, leaves its traces on everything else. At the same time, the world grows smaller: its vastness is encapsulated in a small number of offices with telephones, telexes, and dossiers.

Maigret and Smiley are moral figures par excellence: Le Carré and Simenon are, above all, observers, moralists. Their morality is skeptical, pessimistic, opposed to that faith of Sherlock Holmes's in a limited set of behavioral precepts founded on an unshakeable universe. Le Carré's

From the *Dietari 1979–1982*

novels may be read as apologetics for a very specific historical and social world. Here we must speak again of Balzac, because the impression these two authors give is, at its heart, the same one we get from Balzac: of the repetitive, circular, monotonous, exasperating, vulgar, and predictable presence of evil in human affairs.

Perhaps this is why, like Balzac, Simenon and Le Carré shine in their descriptions of circumstances and surroundings. From the physical environment, from the atmosphere, they create a metaphor of the natural world. And this makes them poets, if a poet is, as Goethe allegedly says, a person who thinks in images. Images of sorrow: streets of somber, dusty cities where we feel alone.

8 May 1980

The Only Emperor

We all know that formerly, Death was a woman with a sickle. The sickle speaks of relentless reaping in the neutral light of silent fields. The Greek poet saw the passage of human lives as a light crackle of falling leaves. Like sheaves of wheat, we await the hour of final silence. Further afield, the reaping goes on into the evening.

Death is also – as in a Book of Hours, vaporous and melancholic – a pale, luxuriant lady with a glimmer of jewels on her cloak. Or the brusque terror of a skeleton kissing a naked maiden, or embracing a matron who offers up the prideful bouquet of lust. At times, Death may be a man: a comely gentleman, dressed in black, seductive, even, like Frederic March in an old film. Sometimes Death is not personified, but is instead the path from this present world to the aqueous one beyond the mirror.

Then, there is a poem by Wallace Stevens that speaks to us of Death in another way. Death? Well, it doesn't *speak* to us anywhere of Death; no one makes us read the poem in this light. Civilised, refined, reticent, the North American poet knew that the complex mechanics of word and image a writer sets in motion are richer if slightly ambiguous. In art, ambiguity is often the sincerest tribute to veracity, because there is a kind of fidelity to truth only obtainable when we have learned to respect the imprecision of lived experience. What is the meaning of those transient minutes of a sonata by Domenico Scarlatti? Everything and nothing, if we ask here of *meaning* consonance with *meaning* of the kind characteristic of a text like the one you are presently reading.

Let us not talk too long, then, about the *meaning* of Wallace Stevens's poem; let us talk instead of what it *says*. And what it says is, briefly, that we human beings may persist, with concupiscent curds, and dresses, and flowers wrapped in newspaper; that we may take things from the dresser and a sheet that will cover a cold, dumb face. We may do these things, but it's all the same, because on this earth, there is only one emperor. And we may imagine this emperor as very cold and very white, or perhaps half-molten and brightly, vividly coloured. Someone gentle and benevolent, a snowman, perhaps. Like the snowman, he has a chummy air about him. But if we approach him, his touch will freeze us. This is the sentence of all empires. Because, the poem says, the only emperor is the emperor of ice cream. Death, the great vendor of ice cream.

13 June 1980

A Sunday in April

This morning, Monsieur Henri Beyle, French consul in Civitavecchia, has gone out for a stroll around Rome. We have grown used to calling him Stendhal. Stendhal wrote books; Monsieur Henri Beyle took walks around Rome, Milan, or Paris; Monsieur Beyle went to the opera; Monsieur Beyle had stormy love affairs. From the imagination and the disquiet and the pain of Monsieur Beyle, the art of Stendhal was born: precise, inalterable, terse. Beneath the radiant and precise tension of words, we feel the heat of flames.

For example, in this note from one Sunday in 1834, when Monsieur Beyle, at evening, takes another of his promenades through Rome. We are on the cusp of spring, 6 April to be exact. Some months before, Monsieur Beyle embarked on an interesting journey. On 15 December, on his way through to Italy, he met a noteworthy couple, two writers from his homeland: the poet Alfred de Musset and the novelist Aurore Dupin, who went by the name of George Sand. Together, the three of them traveled on along the Rhone, with its deep, ample waters, toward the serenity of the Italian sky. If you care to, you may see in Venice, like an immutable chamber amid the sumptuous storm of marble, the room in the Hotel Royal Danielli Excelsior where the poet and his muse lodged. But Beyle's eyes, in that Roman spring, were filled with another, very different splendor. Because, with fervor, those eyes seek a note of richer colour in the placid clarity of the day.

And it is richer, this colour: from afar, it seems to flicker like flames. Monsieur Henri Beyle runs through the people toward that swatch of red. Already he is in the middle of the street; there is a girl who has fallen to the ground. She has just been murdered before the eyes of all. Next to the girl's head, a red pool of spilt blood has formed, as if in an instant. Death, in France, is most often the corollary of violent political passion or financial resentments: a tribute paid to power or to hatred. In Italy, as in the days of the Renaissance, death may still appear in light of an excess of splendor: immoderate luxury of passion and energy, theatrical, sublime, and exalting, like the architecture that distinguishes the country's streets. Or so, at least, it seems so to Monsieur Beyle.

Monsieur Beyle, when he writes, becomes Stendhal. Stendhal

is perhaps fascinating, above all else, for his capacity to establish an equilibrium between acuity of vision and the internal dramaturgy that orders and compels his writing. Returned from his walk, that same afternoon, Monsieur Beyle – Stendhal – writes of the event in the margins of a book, even noting the approximate dimensions of the puddle of blood. He appends a lone commentary: 'This is what Monsieur Hugo calls being bathed in one's own blood.'

Is this insensitivity, sarcasm? No: it is sensitivity in the extreme. It is respect for the real and tangible pool of blood, respect for lived pain, which imposes a moral corrective on rhetoric. To decapitate a cliché is to come close and observe something: the concrete suffering of a girl murdered on a Roman street. Hugo's respect for the word took a different form: magnifying it into monumentality. Thus words maintain a complex moral relation with things lived.

27 June 1980

A Gentleman in Majorca

The first thing that drew my attention was the library, I remember. I had only seen one other like it before. When I used to visit the home of J.V. Foix in Barcelona, I was always surprised by the impeccable, unanimous leather bindings of the Greek and Latin classics published by the Fundació Bernat Metge, exalted in their very noble wrappings. Those books, and a few more, just a few, that he may have loved, were visibly the true center of Foix's moral life. Now, in Majorca, I saw the sun, bright and yellow, singeing or else chiseling the dark green of the olive trees, and the flashes of the sea, of a very pure blue, with a wounding, knifelike glow emerging between the cracks in the promontories. Two friends and I entered a house very different from Foix's. Rustic, with a trail outside, and every room overwhelmed by the light. Less than a site of meditative contemplation, that room gave the impression of a workplace. High shelves bore thick books, well maintained; not classical texts, but Greek and Latin dictionaries and anthologies of myths. There was – if we looked closely – an instinctive communion between the earthy clarity of the landscape and the mythical world throbbing in the heart of those tomes. Archeology as a lived poem.

The house's owner was around seventy-five years old: he received us in the garden with a straw hat on his head. The landscape was a part of him, too: he said he had chosen to live in Deià years before because life there followed the cycles of the crops. The eyes know that there, beyond the warm and shaded clarity of the olive trees, lies the sea, refulgent as the blade of a blue sword or the gleaming of a shield. For the eyes, this means a great deal: this was the world of Homer; this was even the world of Virgil. The appearance of the moon, during the very bright summer nightfall, suggests to us of the white goddess who illuminates his poems.

Will we learn to make of ourselves something akin to the earth, akin to history, akin to the impress of the memory of the gods, akin to the rhythms and cadences that mark the time of life and vision? To see the world, to live the world, not only to live in the world. To live it as this man we were speaking with knew how to live it, this British poet and writer, Robert Graves.

From the *Dietari 1979–1982*

It was already turning dark when he went with us through the garden and out onto the path. A TV reporter filmed him while he spoke vivaciously and at length in his straw hat. Some time back, they had broadcast on television scenes from one of this man's books: *I, Claudius*. Something older than the images, something like the dark root of an olive tree or like the green-glimmering leaf beneath the brilliance of the moon, lit up, with the fractious light of nightfall, the library of Robert Graves in a village in Majorca.

4 July 1980

The Secrets of Plagiarism

In the last volume of his collected works, *Italy and the Mediterranean* – no less intelligent, provocative, and graceful than any of the others – Josep Pla writes: 'The Italian books of Stendhal are pure and simple plagiarism. The anecdotes they contain are magnificent plagiarism. I have always argued that good literature is plagiarism.' Here we are faced with the enigmatic essence of plagiarism. Another writer, more than a century ago, defined it just as well as Pla, a half-Uruguayan, half-Frenchman who died in obscure circumstances and signed his works with the pseudonym Comte de Lautréamont. This young man, on the verge of death, bequeathed to us a series of epigrams and sarcastic *Poésies* which are not poems, but paradoxical aphorisms rendered in prose. Among the most striking of these is the following: 'Plagiarism is necessary. It is already implied in the idea of progress. It clutches the author's sentence, makes use of its expressions, divests it of false ideas, replaces them with right ones.'

And so the swarthy, hallucinatory poet and the arch moralist of Llofriu are in complete agreement about plagiarism. Plagiarism is, at one and the same time, the keystone of literature and its *mysterium magnum*. The plagiarism of plots is unimportant: Phaedra, Medea, Antigone are not anecdotes, but mythical, moral archetypes. The plagiarism of details, of dates, of expressions, is more unsettling, because it may, without a doubt, form the basis of great literature. We could even say that bad literature is merely inept plagiarism, a plagiarism ill-achieved. And good literature?

Good literature, I believe, has discovered the essence of good plagiarism, which, being good, is no longer plagiarism. Good plagiarism recognises in extant literary material a part of the fragmented reality the writer has at his disposal. Shall we take a famous verse of Dante's? Here: *Come neve per le Alpe senza vento*. This is an improvement on a verse by his friend, Guido Cavalcanti: *e bianca neve scender senza vento.* Dante improves its cadence: through the introduction of a deft mention of the Alps, through the elimination of the verb, which suggests the quietude of the landscape. Dante's verse is a re-elaboration that allows us to see with clearer eyes.

Translation, naturally, is not looked upon as plagiarism. But often, it is something more than simply good translation.

I have an anthology, a recent one, of twentieth century Italian poetry. From one of the main contributors, Ungaretti, it includes a translation of a famous sonnet of Góngora's. The translation is elegant, with a crucial last flourish. The beauty of the woman invoked in Góngora's poem vanishes with her death: *into earth, into smoke, into dust, into shadow, into nothing.* Ungaretti translates: *in terra, fumo, polvere, niente.* The shadow is absent. In this change, we see the mark of Ungaretti, the tribute to his individual way of speaking.

A century after Góngora, a Mexican nun – Sor Juana Inés de la Cruz – looked at a portrait of herself to glimpse therein the shadow of death. She concluded, at the end of the sonnet devoted to it: *She is corpse, she is dust, she is shadow, she is nothing.* Here, the model is Góngora once again, but the allusive *earth* and *smoke* are supplanted by the direct vision of the corpse. In its maturity, the baroque becomes more violent and visionary. Would anyone dare speak here of plagiarism?

9 August 1980

Twilight

Is twilight a spectacle? Twilight is scenography. Grazing the river, it is a tender, reddish sword; in the darkening fields, it is the shadow of a red eagle; in the turrets of an ancient city, it is a gargoyle tinged with purple; in the sea, it is another sea, volcanically fused; vanishing in the distance of the broad avenues of capitals, it is a tournament of specters glowing bright on a stellar television. Do we feel alone? More, we feel ourselves. Twilight is a spectacle in the mode of a classical tragedy; a spectacle that casts us into the deepest well of the spirit.

Some time ago, in the drawing room, they finished taking their tea. The conversation was light, voluble, sensible, and trivial; a soft touch of light on the skin of smooth water that quivers and shines. Punctually – the window panes have just begun to redden – the girl comes in announcing: 'Sir, the twilight'. Mr John Ruskin, writer, stands up and goes out to the garden, to witness the slow spectacle of transfiguration.

This other gentleman – perhaps not so different in age – had a rather more active vision of twilight. There is a special, extremely fleeting moment during sundown; on a river, the light blesses the poplars. The poplars are slender, and hold aloft a grille of soft bark and branches and mobile bare leaves. The leaves are green; the sky is deep blue; the twilight is red and ochre. But the eye, at the center of the twilight, communes with a confused and total and transitory apotheosis of splendors.

Fifteen minutes. We have only fifteen minutes of this brilliance that binds the poplars and the twilight. Fifteen minutes at this time of year, then everything goes blurry and black. This gentleman comes every day to see the poplars at the same fleeting and sublime hour. He comes in a fisherman's boat; but it is not a boat like others. It has, scattered inside it, strange contraptions, easel, paintbrushes, colours, an artist's utensils. In 1891, Claude Monet, painter, looked, from one day to the next, at this strange fluvial artifact, the fugitive splendor of the poplars during the final fifteen minutes of twilight.

Painting is an art of the instant; the poem is an art of the instant. Monet's poplars are now in New York. In this inaugural moment of summer, after looking at them for a moment, a poet – Octavio Paz –

From the *Dietari 1979–1982*

has fixed in verse the moment Monet fixed on canvas. Words, colours: mirages that glide and flee. No: still light of what lives in consciousness, like the memory of the clarity of twilight after the full arrival of night.

19 August 1980

Musil, the Spectator

This man, born exactly one hundred years ago today – on 6 November 1880 – this Austrian, Robert Musil – is he the last writer of a prior era, or the first writer of the era we inhabit now? Perhaps he is situated at their point of intersection.

It is not a settled fact that everyday reality and literature have anything to do with each other; neither the Renaissance nor the Baroque era, strictly speaking, assumed as much. Above all because, from the philosophical perspective, reality, in those days, was a volatile appearance; stability was only granted to perennial ideas. And when literature and the real do sustain some kind of relation, this draws, subtly, on the interconnections, the weave of multiple resonances, between external reality – the visible world – and its internal counterpart: the world of the text, which is not a double of the real, but its translation into another order, that of literary fiction. What captivates us, then, is not the world itself, but the world become literature. And this is what occurs in Musil.

Osmosis takes place between the writer and his protagonist, the mathematician Ulrich. Ulrich is the man without qualities, not so much a man without *manly attributes* as one lacking in all that might properly be considered pertinent to a man of the time: a man without properties – not physical, but moral ones – or, to put it otherwise, without characteristics, positive or negative. Ulrich is a neutral, an abstract man: the man of the idea, the idea made man. Ulrich breaks the current, the fabric of the world: while others participate, he observes. He is contemplative, but not passive. Analytical.

Ulrich is, though in a different way, as marginal, as strange, as intensely lucid as K., protagonist of Kafka's major novels. Like K., he lives in a precise historical world: the last days of the Austro-Hungarian Empire. Ritualistic, precise as a metronome, and at the same time bereft of genuine moral substance, this inwardly atrophied world recollects those Parisian ceremonies detailed by Proust. If it strikes us as unusual, this is largely because it crowns a different literary and philosophical tradition, and displaces the center of attention from the specter of the social, even from gradations of consciousness, to home in on the spirit of the age, which finds itself in technophiliac zeal.

It is a beautiful day in August of 1913 in Vienna when he begins *The Man Without Qualities*. The automobiles hurtle by; in an old palace, restored in successive phases, with a garden, lives Ulrich, exempt, disposable, the man without qualities, a spectator and nothing more. He is struggling to calculate, when we meet him for the first time, the immense quantity of energy a man requires to do nothing, to simply resist the psychic shock of living in a big city. The man without qualities has no sense of reality; he is unsuited to practical life. With a watch in his hand, he times the vain traffic on the street. Ten minutes have passed: Ulrich puts aside his watch and laughs. As he passes, he throws a blow at the punching bag hanging from the roof. In Musil's world, actions are like this: violent spasms of futility amid the crude brilliance of the intellect.

6 November 1980

Witches in Venice

There is something not right with this boy – Giacomo Casanova. Blood runs from his nostrils – a bad sign! We are in Venice, in the stifling dog days of summer, when August opens the torrid wings of a door made of embers. It is 1733, and the boy is eight years old. Now is when he feels his intellect awaken: head against the wall, nostrils draining blood. Drop by drop, in clots, deep red on the floor of the room. It is the first recollection of conscious life – years later, convalescing in the library of the castle of Count Waldstein, in the harsh Bohemian winter, all icicles, chill, and solitude – that the old chevalier, Giacomo Casanova de Seingalt, will retain.

Fortunately, the boy with the nosebleeds has a diligent grandmother. Her name is Marcia, like the wife of Cato the Younger, who saw, in the Purgatory of Dante's *Divine Comedy*, the *nobile castello* where the spirits of the virtuous ladies of pagan eras dwelt. Marcia, the grandmother, has something pagan about her as well. When the day darkens, she washes the boy's face with cool water, and without anyone's knowing, sets off with him in a gondola for the island of Murano, dwelling of witches who will find a remedy for the illness that makes him bleed. There is an old woman there seated on a straw pallet, surrounded by black cats.

The grandmother and the witch speak in whispers. A gleaming silver ducat flashes in the hand of the healer, and young Giacomo – stanching the flow of blood from his nose with a handkerchief – is shut up in a box. They take him out, wrap him in a cloth scented with the smoke of mysterious potions; they make him swallow six tablets that resemble sugared almonds, and massage his wrists and the nape of his neck with an odiferous ointment.

That night, when the gondola has returned from Murano and the moon has a wheaten pallor silhouetted against the sky, young Giacomo in his bedroom is roused by the first traces of daylight. A woman emerges from the chimney: in sumptuous clothing, she wears on her head a crown of precious stones that look like fire. With languid majesty, very slowly, she approaches the bedstead; sitting on the cool bedcover, she empties the contents of various phials over the young man's head. She speaks in a murmur, in words never before heard, and closes the scene of bewitchment with a kiss. The next day, the boy's grandmother demands complete discretion. The episode must remain secret.

Lucid – the handwriting in the manuscript is exquisite – but inwardly wounded, the aged Casanova, in the prison of the library, presumes the visit from the nocturnal enchanter was a dream or a masquerade. And yet, from that day, no more blood ran from his nose. And now, old Casanova, evoking the birth of conscious life, recollects those verses of Horace that speak of magical terrors and nocturnal spirits and the prodigies we come across in dreams. He remembers the exotic and tranquil Venice of the paintings of Longhi: salon scenes, with figures like wax sculptures, gentleman draped in vermillion cassocks, ladies in ivory lace or flowered gowns. And in the center of this detailed and minimal world, domestic witchcraft leaves a blotch, vivid as blood, bitter as memory.

18 November 1980

An Interview with Pere Gimerrer
by Adrian Nathan West
2 January 2019

When you began writing in Catalan in the seventies, you frequently addressed the tentative or unfinished nature of Catalan identity, particularly in linguistic terms. In one essay, you remark that Catalan survived suppression under Primo de Rivera and Franco thanks to the language's prestige among the cultured classes.

In verse, I've only rarely looked at these things, once in a bittersweet line in Castell de Puresa (Castle of Purity) – *So many men dead for the gold of a senyera[1] / perhaps for an apocryphal light* – that is a direct allusion. There are others that are more fragmentary. In Tropic of Cancer:

> A final fringe in dark Montjuïc,
> the gloom and smoke of firing squads, the lighthouse, the lapping
>   of water

This was censored in early editions because it was an explicit reference to the shooting of Lluis Companys and others. It's a passing allusion, but its meaning was obvious to readers at the time.

As a language of culture, Catalan reached a very high point, one of the highest in Europe, from the twelfth or thirteenth to the fifteenth century, starting with Ramon Llull and ending with Tirant lo Blanch, Ausias March, and a number of other writers, particularly from Valencia, Joan Roís de Corella, among others. In terms, not of the number of writers, but of their expressive mastery, Catalan literature was one of the most important in Europe. After that, Catalan largely disappears as a language of culture. There are interesting odds and ends from the seventeenth and eighteenth century, but it is not until the nineteenth century that it really reemerges, in a work of singular ambition: *L'Atlàntida* (Atlantis) by Jacint Verdaguer. Leaving aside its peculiar subject – the celebration of the Spanish conquest of America – it represents an effort at modernisation in two senses: as an attempt first

---

1   The *senyera* is the Catalan flag, widely seen as a symbol for the Catalan people.

to reclaim the literary language from the deterioration it had suffered over the course of three centuries, and second to address a kind of aesthetic stagnation. This was a serious task, and not entirely successful: Verdaguer wasn't out of step with the times, but he was working in a language not yet well adapted to his purposes. Joan Maragall, more or less Verdaguer's contemporary, made similar exertions in this direction, but – if we can play a little loose with chronology – both were, like Machado and Unamuno in Spanish, more poets of the nineteenth century than of the twentieth.

The situation only really changes with Carles Riba and J.V. Foix – these were men who wrote the same kind of poetry being written elsewhere in Europe at the time. Riba has many points in common with Rilke. Foix was associated for a time with the futurists, he was a friend of Marinetti's, but he would soon ally with surrealism, with Paul Éluard. Foix's renovation of the language was at once brilliant and quixotic: since Catalan had reached its apogee in the fifteenth century, he chose to take the fifteenth century as his point of departure. And so his poetry is a curious blend of medieval language – not of a grotesque kind, not just choosing any old medieval word, his idiom is not at all artificial in this way – and the language of people from the countryside, in particular from Port de la Selva, where he had a home and would go swim and spend the summers. His expressions resonate with surrealism and with the pure psychic automatism of Breton and Dalí, but you can tease out their meaning looking back to poets like Góngora. He could explain every one of his images to you clearly. Maybe he came up with these explanations after writing them, I don't know, but they were always coherent.

There is a difficulty with Foix: he was allied with the right whereas surrealism – with the marked exception of Dalí – was a movement of the left, and so even if people admire his work, he is a difficult model to follow. Other poets come after him, nurtured by his work as well as by Verdaguer and Maragall. Two, in my judgment, are major writers: Gabriel Ferrater, the only Catalan poet whose work resembles Auden's, and Joan Brossa, who follows in Foix's footsteps, but stripping away the archaisms – writing in the language of everyday people and the working classes, but with completely surreal images. Does that answer the question?

Yes, well…

Now, what all of them are after is very clear: the Catalan language should not only go on existing, but should achieve the same literary distinction it had in the fifteenth century. And that, in my opinion, was something they accomplished even before the war. That proved problematic for Franco. Suppressing a dialect is not the same thing as suppressing a language that is a vehicle of culture. With Catalan, there were all sorts of restrictive measures, but if a person writes like Riba or like Foix, and these things appear in print runs of a hundred copies, well, that's something linguistic politics aren't well equipped to combat. We're not talking about direct militancy in the Neruda manner, but the perpetuation of the language following vanguardist models at a time when the language was prohibited.

> *Catalan is your mother language, but you began writing in Spanish.*
> *Can you talk a bit about your linguistic background?*

I understand mother language to mean the language one learns the names of things in – not all things, obviously. So that came first. Then I was educated in Spanish. This education in Spanish was almost simultaneous with my education in Latin and in French. When I was young, I met Vicente Aleixandre, Octavio Paz, and Rafael Alberti, poets who wrote in Spanish, but at seventeen or eighteen, I also met Foix and Brossa and Ferrater, each of whom traced out very different paths in Catalan. But another thing is, cinema had immense importance for me. If you get used to watching movies in the original, you already live in a multilingual world. When I was thirteen – I'm not making this up – I had the sense that living in Spain at that moment was rather uninteresting, and the easiest thing for me was to pretend I was a French boy from the provinces, and that was the way I would read *Cahiers de cinema*, which was brilliant in those days. This was a mental game of mine, to try and read it as if I were actually in Tours or Rouen – not the capital, but these smaller cities, which produced their own great writers.

> *The theme of cultural backwardness has been important in Spain from the*
> *Generation of '98 up to Carlos Rojas and Juan Benet nearly a century later.*
> *You yourself say of Verdaguer that he was a contemporary of Mallarmé*

*and Rimbaud but patterned his writing on Hugo. When did Catalan
literature catch up with the times?*

More than backwardness, I would call it a chronological imbalance.
You point out Verdaguer, but I wouldn't saddle him with this, this is
a generalised problem in Spain and in Spanish poetry in America –
not so much in Portuguese, the evolution of Portuguese and Brazilian
literature is different for any number of reasons. The pattern starts to
undo itself with Rubén Darió in America and, not long afterward,
with Juan Ramón Jiménez in Spain. It's significant that Darío, when
he publishes his most cosmopolitan book, *Los Raros*, which examines
a number of European figures, had not yet been to Europe: everything
he discusses he has either read or knows from photographs and prints.
With him and with Juan Ramón Jiménez we enter an aesthetic era that
marks a break with Verdaguer or Machado or Unamuno.

*In your book on Tàpies, you say that modern art is defined by the
disappearance of theme as an external motif – by the dissolution of the
traditional hierarchy of motifs. Is your poetry modern in this sense?*

This theme of the disappearance of the exterior, that isn't really my
phrase, it's an idea from André Breton. Breton saw the disappearance
of the exterior as pertaining above all to poetry; it is apparent in some
ways in the plastic arts as well, but distinctly, because surrealist art
remained figurative, if not realistic.

As to whether this applies to my own poetry, the relation is a
bit strange. My poetry has passed through many stages. I've never
considered it classical; there were times when I have attempted to grant
it a semblance of classicism, but only a semblance; whole books of mine
give this impression, but their internal functioning isn't classical – it's
as if they were a pastiche of classical poetry serving to conceal a modern
approach. There are precedents for this, Fernando Pessoa, for example,
did this in several languages.

*Does the eroticism of your poetry correspond to what Octavio Paz calls 'the
rebellion of the body'?*

Paz says that in an important book, *Conjunctions and Disjunctions*, in a
study of the Rokeby Venus of Velazquez. This is the only painting of

An Interview with Pere Gimerrer

its type by Velazquez, and was a private commission, probably for the Count-Duke of Olivares. There is a mirror in the painting, remember? And the most intriguing aspect is compositional, the way the mirror reveals this strange symmetry between the buttocks of the Venus and the face in the mirror, which we don't see. Octavio Paz dilates on this at great length. It was a topic that concerned him at the end of the seventies, and is clearly related to the social changes we all know as well as aspects of surrealism, with which Paz had deep contacts, he corresponded with Breton, knew Benjamin Peret in Mexico, Miró, and so on. This symmetry does have a certain importance for me.

Can you say something about the influence of Ramon Llull on your work?

Ramon Llull is a difficult figure to grasp. Leaving aside his ontological, philosophical orientation, and his enormous importance for the language – despite being the first to really write literature in Catalan, he does it with utter mastery... leaving this aside, he possesses an extraordinary visionary momentum. If you're not immersed in his world, maybe you don't understand what each of his phrases means, but their force still comes across. 'No man is visible', don't ask me what it means, to all appearances it's the very opposite of true. Claudio Guillén discusses that quote in relation my book *Fortuny*, drawing a parallel between Llull's 'No man is visible' and my own phrase, 'The eye denies to the eye the vision in the eye's depths.' I can't say there is a direct influence because he is from a different world, Lull is a medieval theologian. But the impact of his images themselves is exceptional.

You have remarked, about writing in several languages, that the choice is not conscious, that certain rhythms suggest certain languages and vice versa.

Well, many writers have written in different languages, look at Ezra Pound. In theory, he wrote in English. Still, large parts of his books aren't in English. A better example is Pessoa. Not only did he write in Portuguese, English and French, but in these languages, he was four or five different poets. I haven't tried to establish heteronyms proper like Pessoa, but I have at times attempted to differentiate the personae writing my poems, to keep them from seeming too similar, and language does play a role here. I don't know as many languages as

I would like, but I read in eight or nine, and doing so inclines you to try them out. I wrote a *plaquette* in French and a fair bit of prose, one book in Italian, everything else is Spanish and Catalan, I haven't tried my hand at others.

So no book in English?

No book in English, in Portuguese, even less in Latin, which is the language I have studied most. Well, you can never say, I hadn't planned to write a book in Italian, but one day I did. I don't think I would write in Portuguese, Provençal, or English, but I don't know, it depends on the circumstances. I wrote the Italian book in at a time when I was travelling to Italy, I had been reading a lot of Italian literature and watching Italian films, I don't know if this could happen with English or Portuguese, but I can't rule it out.

Is your poetry abstract?

I don't know. I hadn't thought about it. What makes you ask?

I suppose there are two ways to interpret poetry. If it's abstract, there's not really a hermeneutic entryway, but if not, the reader has to look for those clues, try to understand…

This is a question that can be traced back to a specific moment, when Rimbaud, in *Illuminations* and *A Season in Hell,* does something no one had done before, or not rigorously: he treats words as a painter treats colour, or as a musician treats sounds. As abstractions, in other words, for their plastic, sonic, visual qualities. And many people follow in his footsteps. This idea, which he perhaps didn't formulate coherently, is astonishing: he opens a road to a place where words no longer matter semantically, and you have to make an effort to forget what they mean in normal or philosophical language; he treats them like sounds or colours, and this even makes you see the painting and the music that came before them in a new way. This was revolutionary, and its effects are evident in certain of my poems, where allusions don't need to be tracked down, but instead serve a kind of atmospheric purpose.

Index of Titles

Afterward   64
The American Poet   97
Apotheosis   73
Apparitions   47
The Bedroom of the Poetess   104
Beginnings   106
Bell   65
Blind Fire   19
Ceremonies   76
Compact   80
Death   62
Deserted Space   30
Desire   67
Distant   12
Elegy   14
End   77
The Enemy Within   89
Evening   78
Exile   70
Facts and Morals   95
Fate   58
A Gentleman in Majorca   114
The Gloaming Hour   71
I am Still Learning   84
Land of Antoni Tàpies   46
Landscape   61
Lay   81
Le Carré and Simenon   108
Light of Velintonia   45
May   22
Memories   59
Midday   66
Morn   79
The Mulatta and the Dandy   101

Musil, the Spectator 120
Night in April 28
Now the Poet Undertakes a Practical Act 11
The Only Emperor 110
Philistines 63
The Pistol and the Drawing Rooms 99
Plaint 72
The Poet and the Dictator 83
Poetic Art 56
A Russian in Paris 87
Sculpture 57
Second Vision of March 4
The Secrets of Plagiarism 116
Sign 68
Simulacra 93
Snares 1
Solstice 23
A Sorcerer's Disappearance 85
Spectacle 69
Stalking 74
A Sunday in April 112
Systems 3
Testament 75
Time 54
A Toast 91
Tropic of Capricorn 7
Twilight 118
Unity 27
Vigil 60
Vision 24
Vlad Drakul 16
Winter 55
Witches in Venice 122